Listening & Speaking **3**

A Revised Edition of
Authentic & Aware

• •

Karen Carlisi

Susana Christie

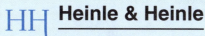
Heinle & Heinle
Thomson Learning™

Australia • Canada • Denmark • Japan • Mexico
New Zealand • Philippines • Puerto Rico • Singapore
Spain • United Kingdom • United States

For Christopher and Emma

Developmental Editors: Jennifer Monaghan, Jill Korey O'Sullivan
Sr. Production Coordinator: Maryellen E. Killeen
Market Development Director: Charlotte Sturdy
Sr. Manufacturing Coordinator: Mary Beth Hennebury
Interior Design: Julia Gecha
Illustrations: Pre-Press Company, Inc., Len Shalansky
Photo Research: Jeffrey M. Freeland

Cover Design: Ha Nguyen Design
Cover Images: PhotoDisc®
Composition/Production: Pre-Press Company, Inc.
Freelance Production Editor: Janet McCartney
Copyeditor: Donald Pharr
Printer/Binder: Bawden

For permission to use material from this text, contact us:
web   www.thomsonrights.com
fax   1-800-730-2215
phone 1-800-730-2214

For photo credits, see page 246.

Heinle & Heinle Publishers
20 Park Plaza
Boston, MA 02116

UK/EUROPE/MIDDLE EAST:
Thomson Learning
Berkshire House
168-173 High Holborn
London, WC1V 7AA, United Kingdom

AUSTRALIA/NEW ZEALAND:
Nelson/Thomson Learning
102 Dodds Street
South Melbourne
Victoria 3205 Australia

CANADA:
Nelson/Thomson Learning
1120 Birchmount Road
Scarborough, Ontario
Canada M1K 5G4

LATIN AMERICA:
Thomson Learning
Seneca, 53
Colonia Polanco
11560 México D.F. México

ASIA (excluding Japan):
Thomson Learning
60 Albert Street #15-01
Albert Complex
Singapore 189969

JAPAN:
Thomson Learning
Palaceside Building, 5F
1-1-1 Hitotsubashi, Chiyoda-ku
Tokyo 100 0003, Japan

SPAIN:
Thomson Learning
Calle Magallanes, 25
28015-Madrid
España

Library of Congress Cataloging-in-Publication Data
Carlisi, Karen.
  Tapestry listening & speaking 3 / Karen Carlisi, Susana Christie.
    p. cm.
  ISBN 0-8384-0023-X (alk. paper)
  1. English language—Textbooks for foreign speakers. 2. English language—Spoken
English—Problems, exercises, etc. 3. Listening—Problems, exercises, etc. I. Title:
Tapestry listening and speaking three. II. Christie, Susana. III. Title.

PE1128 .C36 2000
428.3'4—dc21   99-054093

 This book is printed on acid-free recycled paper.

Printed in the United States of America.
1 2 3 4 5 6 7 8 9 03 02 01 00 99

A VERY SPECIAL THANK YOU

The publisher and authors would like to thank the following coordinators and instructors who have offered many helpful insights and suggestions for change throughout the development of the new *Tapestry*.

Alicia Aguirre, *Cañada College*
Fred Allen, *Mission College*
Maya Alvarez-Galvan, *University of Southern California*
Geraldine Arbach, *Collège de l'Outaouais, Canada*
Dolores Avila, *Pasadena City College*
Sarah Bain, *Eastern Washington University*
Kate Baldus, *San Francisco State University*
Fe Baran, *Chabot College*
Gail Barta, *West Valley College*
Karen Bauman, *Biola University*
Liza Becker, *Mt. San Antonio College*
Leslie Biaggi, *Miami-Dade Community College*
Andrzej Bojarczak, *Pasadena City College*
Nancy Boyer, *Golden West College*
Glenda Bro, *Mt. San Antonio College*
Brooke Brummitt, *Palomar College*
Linda Caputo, *California State University, Fresno*
Alyce Campbell, *Mt. San Antonio College*
Barbara Campbell, *State University of New York, Buffalo*
Robin Carlson, *Cañada College*
Ellen Clegg, *Chapman College*
Karin Cintron, *Aspect ILS*
Diane Colvin, *Orange Coast College*
Martha Compton, *University of California, Irvine*
Nora Dawkins, *Miami-Dade Community College*
Beth Erickson, *University of California, Davis*
Charles Estus, *Eastern Michigan University*
Gail Feinstein Forman, *San Diego City College*
Jeffra Flaitz, *University of South Florida*
Kathleen Flynn, *Glendale Community College*
Ann Fontanella, *City College of San Francisco*
Sally Gearhart, *Santa Rosa Junior College*
Alice Gosak, *San José City College*
Kristina Grey, *Northern Virginia Community College*
Tammy Guy, *University of Washington*
Gail Hamilton, *Hunter College*
Patty Heiser, *University of Washington*
Virginia Heringer, *Pasadena City College*
Catherine Hirsch, *Mt. San Antonio College*

Helen Huntley, *West Virginia University*
Nina Ito, *California State University, Long Beach*
Patricia Jody, *University of South Florida*
Diana Jones, *Angloamericano, Mexico*
Loretta Joseph, *Irvine Valley College*
Christine Kawamura, *California State University, Long Beach*
Gregory Keech, *City College of San Francisco*
Kathleen Keesler, *Orange Coast College*
Daryl Kinney, *Los Angeles City College*
Maria Lerma, *Orange Coast College*
Mary March, *San José State University*
Heather McIntosh, *University of British Columbia, Canada*
Myra Medina, *Miami-Dade Community College*
Elizabeth Mejia, *Washington State University*
Cristi Mitchell, *Miami-Dade Community College*
Sylvette Morin, *Orange Coast College*
Blanca Moss, *El Paso Community College*
Karen O'Neill, *San José State University*
Bjarne Nielsen, *Central Piedmont Community College*
Katy Ordon, *Mission College*
Luis Quesada, *Miami-Dade Community College*
Gustavo Ramírez Toledo, *Colegio Cristóbol Colón, Mexico*
Nuha Salibi, *Orange Coast College*
Alice Savage, *North Harris College*
Dawn Schmid, *California State University, San Marcos*
Mary Kay Seales, *University of Washington*
Denise Selleck, *City College of San Francisco*
Gail Slater, *Brooklyn and Staten Island Superintendency*
Susanne Spangler, *East Los Angeles College*
Karen Stanley, *Central Piedmont Community College*
Sara Storm, *Orange Coast College*
Margaret Teske, *ELS Language Centers*
Maria Vargas-O'Neel, *Miami-Dade Community College*
James Wilson, *Mt. San Antonio College and Pasadena City College*
Karen Yoshihara, *Foothill College*

ACKNOWLEDGMENTS

Thanks to Howard Hertz, Marty Huang, Shelagh Rose, and Andrew Cho.
Special thanks to Jennifer Monaghan.

Tapestry Listening & Speaking 3: Contents

ACADEMIC POWER STRATEGIES	CNN VIDEO CLIPS	PRONUNCIATION: THE SOUND OF IT	LISTENING OPPORTUNITIES
Survive the beginning of the school year by paying attention to details and asking for help.	"Freshmen Fears" A student discusses the issues he faces as he starts his freshman year at a large university in the United States.	Pronunciation of prepositions	A conversation between a student and an academic advisor A conversation between two students discussing the beginning of the college semester A lecture given by a college professor on the first day of class
Contribute your ideas in group activities.	"The Bilingual Storyteller" A teacher uses storytelling to help his students feel more comfortable living in a culture that is different from their native culture.	Reductions in conversation	A conversation between two people about going out to dinner Two people talk about studying in other countries
Plan in advance in order to get the most out of each class session.	"Anti-Divorce Class" To resolve marital problems, couples attend a workshop designed to prevent divorce.	Stressed syllables	Four dialogues, each with a different misunderstanding or breakdown in communication Three people discuss their communication problems with members of the opposite sex
Cooperate with classmates during group work.	"The Ellis Island Decision" A discussion of the United States Supreme Court decision about the political boundaries of the historical landmark, Ellis Island.	Distinguishing syllables and recognizing reductions	Five short conversations—focusing on the speakers' volume, tone, and intent A lecture about conflict resolution Two students discuss their views on boundaries
Increase your success as a student and a language learner by improving your ability to remember.	"Cracking Down on the Homeless" Residents and homeless people in the Berkeley area talk about the problem of homelessness.	Guessing meaning from intonation	An interview about financial planning A conversation between two students talking about the high cost of education

ACADEMIC POWER STRATEGIES	CNN VIDEO CLIPS	PRONUNCIATION: THE SOUND OF IT	LISTENING OPPORTUNITIES
Make an effort to see how your learning relates to what is happening in the world around you.	"Do We Really Need to Know?" A debate about whether or not the press should reveal private information about politicians.	Conversational pauses	A debate about TV censorship vs. people's rights and freedoms A journalist gives his opinion about the public's right to know vs. public figures' right to privacy
Search for ideas that challenge your own.	"Teaching Character" An elementary school has begun a program to teach character to children.	Correct stress placement	A person talks about good behavior and what he was taught about ethics in school Two dialogues between people discussing solutions and alternatives
Learn to talk about uncomfortable subjects with greater comfort and confidence.	"Two Sides to Cloning" Three people give their viewpoints on the pros and cons of human cloning.	Using intonation to emphasize different points of view	A radio talk show in which two doctors debate the moral issues concerning technology and medical experimentation A pregnant woman talks about the pros and cons of medical advances in pre-natal testing
Develop realistic plans and prioritize them.	"An Ecovillage" The story of a village created to decrease the amount of harm to the environment.	Understanding reductions	A discussion on talk radio between an environmentalist and a caller about the impact of technology on the environment A conversation between two students with contrasting viewpoints about what makes a good study environment
Manage the stress of academic deadlines, tests, and schedules.	"Student Stress" A comparison of the stress level for students in the United States, Japan, and China.	Prepositions with two-word verbs Recognizing "filler" sounds and words	A discussion on talk radio about stress management A student and a full-time working person talk about the stress in their lives

Welcome to TAPESTRY!

Empower your students with the **Tapestry Listening & Speaking** series!

Language learning can be seen as an ever-developing tapestry woven with many threads and colors. The elements of the tapestry are related to different language skills such as listening and speaking, reading, and writing; the characteristics of the teachers; the desires, needs, and backgrounds of the students; and the general second language development process. When all of these elements are working together harmoniously, the result is a colorful, continuously growing tapestry of language competence of which the student and the teacher can be proud.

Tapestry is built upon a framework of concepts that helps students become proficient in English and prepared for the academic and social challenges in college and beyond. The following principles underlie the instruction provided in all of the components of the **Tapestry** program:

- Empowering students to be responsible for their learning
- Using Language Learning Strategies and Academic Power Strategies to enhance one's learning, both in and out of the classroom
- Offering motivating activities that recognize a variety of learning styles
- Providing authentic and meaningful input to heighten learning and communication
- Learning to understand and value different cultures
- Integrating language skills to increase communicative competence
- Providing goals and ongoing self-assessment to monitor progress

Guide to **Tapestry Listening & Speaking**

Setting Goals focuses students' attention on the learning they will do in each chapter.

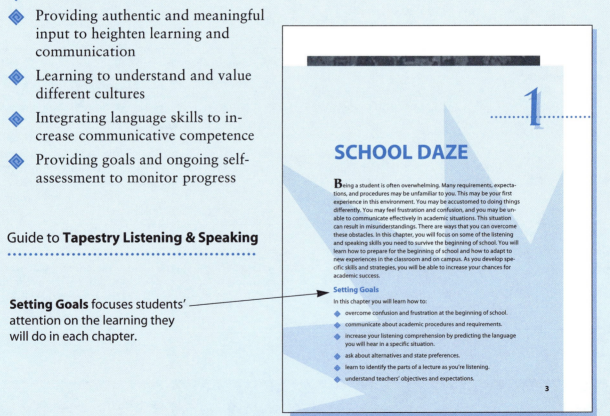

1

SCHOOL DAZE

Being a student is often overwhelming. Many requirements, expectations, and procedures may be unfamiliar to you. This may be your first experience in this environment. You may be accustomed to doing things differently. You may feel frustration and confusion, and you may be unable to communicate effectively in academic situations. This situation can result in misunderstandings. There are ways that you can overcome these obstacles. In this chapter, you will focus on some of the listening and speaking skills you need to survive the beginning of school. You will learn how to prepare for the beginning of school and how to adapt to new experiences in the classroom and on campus. As you develop specific skills and strategies, you will be able to increase your chances for academic success.

Setting Goals

In this chapter you will learn how to:

- overcome confusion and frustration at the beginning of school.
- communicate about academic procedures and requirements.
- increase your listening comprehension by predicting the language you will hear in a specific situation.
- ask about alternatives and state preferences.
- learn to identify the parts of a lecture as you're listening.
- understand teachers' objectives and expectations.

3

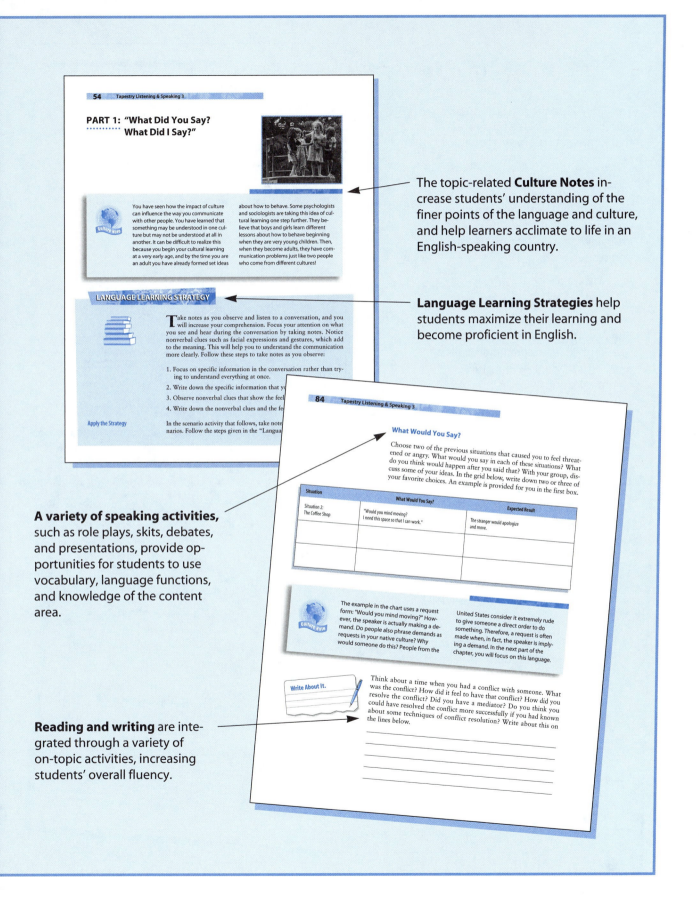

PART 1: "What Did You Say? What Did I Say?"

Culture Note

You have seen how the impact of culture can influence the way you communicate with other people. You have learned that something may be understood in one culture but may not be understood at all in another. It can be difficult to realize this because you begin your cultural learning at a very early age, and by the time you are an adult you have already formed set ideas about how to behave. Some psychologists and sociologists are taking this idea of cultural learning one step further. They believe that boys and girls learn different lessons about how to behave beginning when they are very young children. Then, when they become adults, they have communication problems just like two people who come from different cultures!

LANGUAGE LEARNING STRATEGY

Take notes as you observe and listen to a conversation, and you will increase your comprehension. Focus your attention on what you see and hear during the conversation by taking notes. Notice nonverbal clues such as facial expressions and gestures, which add to the meaning. This will help you to understand the communication more clearly. Follow these steps to take notes as you observe:

1. Focus on specific information in the conversation rather than trying to understand everything at once.
2. Write down the specific information that yo[...]
3. Observe nonverbal clues that show the feel[...]
4. Write down the nonverbal clues and the fe[...]

Apply the Strategy

In the scenario activity that follows, take note[...] narios. Follow the steps given in the "Langua[...]

The topic-related **Culture Notes** increase students' understanding of the finer points of the language and culture, and help learners acclimate to life in an English-speaking country.

Language Learning Strategies help students maximize their learning and become proficient in English.

What Would You Say?

Choose two of the previous situations that caused you to feel threatened or angry. What would you say in each of these situations? What do you think would happen after you said that? With your group, discuss some of your ideas. In the grid below, write down two or three of your favorite choices. An example is provided for you in the first box.

Situation	What Would You Say?	
		Expected Result
Situation 2: The Coffee Shop	"Would you mind moving? I need this space so that I can work."	The stranger would apologize and move.

Culture Note

The example in the chart uses a request form: "Would you mind moving?" However, the speaker is actually making a demand. Do people also phrase demands as requests in your native culture? Why would someone do this? People from the United States consider it extremely rude to give someone a direct order to do something. Therefore, a request is often made when, in fact, the speaker is implying a demand. In the next part of the chapter, you will focus on this language.

Write About It.

Think about a time when you had a conflict with someone. What was the conflict? How did it feel to have that conflict? How did you resolve the conflict? Did you have a mediator? Do you think you could have resolved the conflict more successfully if you had known about some techniques of conflict resolution? Write about this on the lines below.

_____

_____

_____

_____

_____

A variety of speaking activities, such as role plays, skits, debates, and presentations, provide opportunities for students to use vocabulary, language functions, and knowledge of the content area.

Reading and writing are integrated through a variety of on-topic activities, increasing students' overall fluency.

Tapestry Threads provide students with interesting facts and quotes that jumpstart classroom discussions.

Engaging listening selections provide authentic news broadcasts, interviews, conversations, debates, and stories.

The Sound of It refines listening, speaking, and pronunciation skills, and helps students gain confidence communicating in English.

Academic Power Strategies give students the knowledge and skills to become successful, independent learners.

Apply the Strategy activities encourage students to take charge of their learning and use their new skills and strategies.

CNN® video clips provide authentic input and further develop listening and speaking skills.

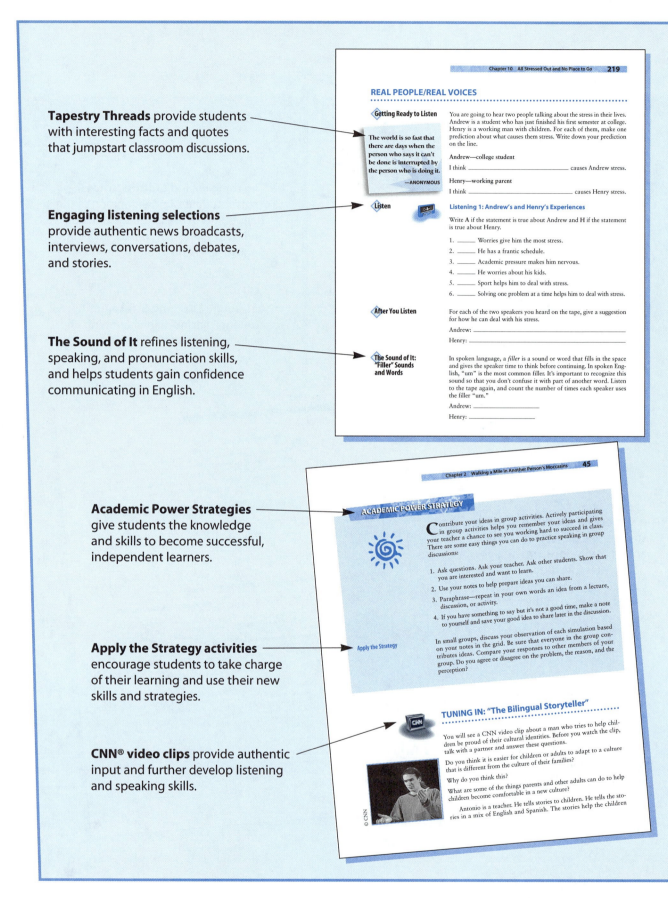

REAL PEOPLE/REAL VOICES

Getting Ready to Listen

> The world is so fast that there are days when the person who says it can't be done is interrupted by the person who is doing it.
> —ANONYMOUS

You are going to hear two people talking about the stress in their lives. Andrew is a student who has just finished his first semester at college. Henry is a working man with children. For each of them, make one prediction about what causes them stress. Write down your prediction on the line.

Andrew—college student

I think _____ causes Andrew stress.

Henry—working parent

I think _____ causes Henry stress.

Listen

Listening 1: Andrew's and Henry's Experiences

Write A if the statement is true about Andrew and H if the statement is true about Henry.

1. _____ Worries give him the most stress.
2. _____ He has a frantic schedule.
3. _____ Academic pressure makes him nervous.
4. _____ He worries about his kids.
5. _____ Sport helps him to deal with stress.
6. _____ Solving one problem at a time helps him to deal with stress.

After You Listen

For each of the two speakers you heard on the tape, give a suggestion for how he can deal with his stress.

Andrew: _____

Henry: _____

The Sound of It: "Filler" Sounds and Words

In spoken language, a *filler* is a sound or word that fills in the space and gives the speaker time to think before continuing. In spoken English, "um" is the most common filler. It's important to recognize this sound so that you don't confuse it with part of another word. Listen to the tape again, and count the number of times each speaker uses the filler "um."

Andrew: _____

Henry: _____

ACADEMIC POWER STRATEGY

Contribute your ideas in group activities. Actively participating in group activities helps you remember your ideas and gives your teacher a chance to see you working hard to succeed in class. There are some easy things you can do to practice speaking in group discussions:

1. Ask questions. Ask your teacher. Ask other students. Show that you are interested and want to learn.
2. Use your notes to help prepare ideas you can share.
3. Paraphrase—repeat in your own words an idea from a lecture, discussion, or activity.
4. If you have something to say but it's not a good time, make a note to yourself and save your good idea to share later in the discussion.

Apply the Strategy

In small groups, discuss your observation of each simulation based on your notes in the grid. Be sure that everyone in the group contributes ideas. Compare your responses to other members of your group. Do you agree or disagree on the problem, the reason, and the perception?

TUNING IN: "The Bilingual Storyteller"

You will see a CNN video clip about a man who tries to help children be proud of their cultural identities. Before you watch the clip, talk with a partner and answer these questions.

Do you think it is easier for children or adults to adapt to a culture that is different from the culture of their families?

Why do you think this?

What are some of the things parents and other adults can do to help children become comfortable in a new culture?

Antonio is a teacher. He tells stories to children. He tells the stories in a mix of English and Spanish. The stories help the children

Test-Taking Tips offer students practical steps for improving their test results.

Check Your Progress helps students monitor their own progress.

Test-Taking Tip

Work with a partner to prepare for speaking-based tests. Practice speaking with your partner about subjects you think you may be asked about on the test. First, one of you can play the part of the "interviewer" while the other takes the role of the "interviewee;" then you can reverse roles. The interviewer should prepare questions to ask before the practice interview begins.

CHECK YOUR PROGRESS

On a scale of 1 to 5, where 1 means "not at all," 2 means "not very well," 3 means "moderately well," 4 means "well," and 5 means "very well," rate how well you have mastered the goals set at the beginning of the chapter:

1 2 3 4 5   overcome confusion and frustration at the beginning of school.

1 2 3 4 5   communicate about academic procedures and requirements.

1 2 3 4 5   increase listening comprehension by predicting the language in a specific situation.

1 2 3 4 5   ask about alternatives and state preferences.

1 2 3 4 5   learn to identify the parts of a lecture while listening.

1 2 3 4 5   understand teachers' objectives and expectations.

If you've given yourself a 3 or lower on any of these goals:

- visit the *Tapestry* web site for additional practice.
- ask your instructor for extra help.
- review the sections of the chapter that you found difficult.
- work with a partner or study group to further your progress.

Expand your classroom at Tapestry Online
www.tapestry.heinle.com
- Online Quizzes
- Instructor's Manuals
- Opportunities to use and expand the Academic Power Strategies
- More!

For a well-integrated curriculum, try the **Tapestry Reading** series and the **Tapestry Writing** series, also from Heinle & Heinle.

To learn more about the **Tapestry** principles, read *The Tapestry of Language Learning,* Second Edition, by Rebecca L. Oxford and Robin C. Scarcella, also from Heinle & Heinle Publishers. ISBN 0-8384-0994-6.

This photo shows students at a university on the first day of school. Usually, the first week of school is very busy and stressful. Students have to be sure that they get the classes they want. They need to buy books and materials that are required for their classes. During the first week, they also find out what is required for each course and how demanding the classes will be. Students may decide to drop a class and add a different class in its place. Look at the photo and think about the difficulties these students face at the beginning of school. What are some of these difficulties, and what can be done about them? Discuss these questions with your classmates.

SCHOOL DAZE

Being a student is often overwhelming. Many requirements, expectations, and procedures may be unfamiliar to you. This may be your first experience in this environment. You may be accustomed to doing things differently. You may feel frustration and confusion, and you may be unable to communicate effectively in academic situations. This situation can result in misunderstandings. There are ways that you can overcome these obstacles. In this chapter, you will focus on some of the listening and speaking skills you need to survive the beginning of school. You will learn how to prepare for the beginning of school and how to adapt to new experiences in the classroom and on campus. As you develop specific skills and strategies, you will be able to increase your chances for academic success.

Setting Goals

In this chapter you will learn how to:

◈ overcome confusion and frustration at the beginning of school.

◈ communicate about academic procedures and requirements.

◈ increase your listening comprehension by predicting the language you will hear in a specific situation.

◈ ask about alternatives and state preferences.

◈ identify the parts of a lecture as you're listening.

◈ understand teachers' objectives and expectations.

Getting Started

Complete the following statements. There are no right or wrong answers. The purpose of this activity is to examine your beliefs, attitudes, and feelings. After you have completed the statements by yourself, discuss your answers with a partner.

What Do I Know About the Topic?

1. Before the first week of school, I should . . .

2. During the first week of school, I should . . .

3. By the end of the first week of school, I will . . .

4. On the first day of a new class, the teacher will usually . . .

5. Some of the things that can confuse or frustrate me during the first week of school are . . .

6. If I get confused or frustrated, I should . . .

7. After the first day of class, if I think the class will be too difficult for me, I should . . .

What Do I Know About the Language?

1. Some words or expressions that I can use to talk about school life are _____

   _____

2. If I want to ask about alternatives to a choice I'm given, I can say

   _____

   _____

3. If I want to state a preference, I can say_____

   _____

In colleges and universities in the United States, students have many choices about the subjects they study, their class schedule, and the teachers of their classes. In this way, students can create a schedule that is most suitable for them. They can also fulfill the requirements of their degree. Therefore, students carry most of the responsibility for managing their academic life, although academic advisors are available to help them. Is this different from your native culture? In your native culture, how much choice do students have in classes, teachers, and times of classes?

PART 1: Communicating About Academic Procedures and Requirements

LANGUAGE YOU CAN USE: ASKING ABOUT ALTERNATIVES/STATING PREFERENCES

Because there are many choices to make at the beginning of a semester, it is useful to know how to ask about the alternatives you may have. It is also useful to know how to state your preferences about the alternatives. Study the expressions and the examples given below for these language functions.

ASKING ABOUT ALTERNATIVES

If I can't . . . , will it be possible to . . . ?

What if . . . ? Will I be able to . . . ?

Do you know of any other . . . ?

EXAMPLES

If I can't get into the 8:00 class, **will it be possible to** take another class?

What if I can't pass this class? **Will I be able to** repeat it?

Do you know of any other classes that are open?

STATING PREFERENCES

I would much rather . . . than . . .

I prefer to . . . so that . . .

I think it's much better for me to . . . than to . . .

EXAMPLES

I would much rather drop the class **than** take the chance of failing it.

I prefer to stay in the class **so that** I can improve my skills.

I think it's much better for me to drop the class **than to** fail it.

USING NEW LANGUAGE

Asking About Alternatives

For each of the situations below, use the expressions from page 5 to ask about the alternatives.

1. You need to pass a test to take the ESL class you want. However, there are other ESL classes listed in the catalogue which may not require that you pass the test. Ask your academic advisor about the alternatives.

   _____

   _____

> **It is the mark of an educated man to be able to entertain a thought without accepting it.**
>
> **—ARISTOTLE**

2. You want to register for a biology class to fulfill a requirement for units in science, but you don't know if it's open. There are other science classes that would fulfill the same requirement. Ask your academic advisor about the alternatives.

   _____

   _____

3. Your academic advisor recommends a sociology professor because the professor has a good understanding of students' needs. However, your advisor isn't sure that the professor's class is open for additional students.

   _____

   _____

4. You are in the bookstore buying a textbook for a class. You don't know about the return policy if you drop the class. Ask the cashier about the alternatives.

   _____

   _____

Stating Preferences

Directions: For each of the situations below, use the expressions from the chart on page 5 to state your preference.

1. There are only two English composition classes open. For one, you've heard that there are few assignments but the teacher is not very good. For the other, you've heard that the teacher is excellent but she gives a lot of assignments.

   _____

   _____

2. It is the second week of school. You don't think you can pass your calculus class. You could drop the class immediately, or you could talk to the teacher about your situation.

   _____

   _____

3. You tried to get into a history class that you really want. You have heard that the professor is very good. When you went to the class, the professor told you that the class is full. The professor said that you should check back in a week because some students may drop the class. You really need to take this class now to fulfill a requirement. There are other sections of the class open. You could wait and try to get into this class or register for another class before it's too late.

   _____

   _____

4. You are trying desperately to get into a class with a professor who has a very good reputation. You could talk to her in her classroom after her class, or you could go try to find her in her office.

   _____

   _____

5. At the beginning of your English composition class, your professor tells you that you're going to have difficulty passing because your writing skills are weak. You could get a tutor through the learning assistance center, or you could drop the class.

   _____

   _____

TALKING TO AN ADVISOR

◆ **Getting Ready to Listen**   Read and discuss the "Academic Power Strategy" below.

ACADEMIC POWER STRATEGY

Survive the beginning of the school year by paying attention to details and asking for help. Students often experience feelings of confusion and frustration at the beginning of the semester. They feel dazed because of the various decisions that must be made and the number of details that need attention. Here are some specific suggestions to help you avoid becoming overwhelmed by these feelings:

1. Pay attention to details.

2. When you are confused, ask for help or clarification from a teacher, an academic advisor, or another student.

3. Find out where teachers' offices are located and look for teachers during their office hours.

4. Always try to solve problems rather than give up.

Apply the Strategy   Now think of an example situation for each of the suggestions. The first one is done for you.

EXAMPLE: Suggestion 1: (Pay attention to details) If a professor tells me to buy the second edition of the textbook rather than the first edition, I should be sure to buy the correct edition even if they look the same.

Example Situations

Suggestion 1: (Pay Attention to Details) _____

_____

_____

Suggestion 2: (Ask for Help) _____

_____

_____

Suggestion 3: (Office Hours) _____

_____

_____

Suggestion 4: (Solve Problems) _____

_____

_____

 Listen

Listening 1: Talking to an Advisor

You will hear a conversation between a student, Soo-Jin, and an academic advisor. The conversation is about a problem Soo-Jin has at school. As you listen, place a check next to the reasons why Soo-Jin is frustrated.

1. _____ She doesn't like her teacher.

2. _____ She was dropped from her ESL class.

3. _____ She didn't have an add slip.

4. _____ Her ESL class is too full.

5. _____ Her English skills are too low for the class.

6. _____ She needs to take the ESL class this semester.

7. _____ Her academic plans are ruined.

8. _____ She doesn't know how to solve her problem.

9. _____ Her professor wouldn't talk to her about the problem.

10. _____ Her professor likes the other students better than her.

◆ After You Listen

With a partner, discuss the reasons why Soo-Jin is frustrated. Then review the suggestions from the "Academic Power Strategy" and discuss how she didn't apply each of them.

A. Reasons: _____

_____

_____

_____

B. Suggestions

1. Pay attention to details.

2. When you are confused, ask for help or clarification from a teacher, an academic advisor, or another student.

3. Find out where teachers' offices are located and look for teachers during their office hours.

4. Always try to solve problems rather than give up.

PROBLEM SOLVING

Below are a number of problems you might have at the beginning of school. For each situation, decide which suggestions from the "Academic Power Strategy" you would use to solve the problem. Then discuss how you would apply those suggestions to the situation.

> **The test of a first-rate intelligence is the ability to hold two opposed ideas in mind at the same time and still retain the ability to function.**
>
> **—F. SCOTT FITZGERALD**

a. Pay attention to details.

b. When you are confused, ask for help or clarification from a teacher, an academic advisor, or another student.

c. Find out where teachers' offices are located and look for teachers during their office hours.

d. Always try to solve problems rather than give up.

1. You bought a textbook from the bookstore for a class you registered for. However, after the first two weeks of the class, you realize that you should drop the class because it is too difficult. You lost the receipt for the book, and the bookstore policy states that you need a receipt in order to return textbooks.

2. You have been in your history class for three weeks. You have a very uncomfortable feeling about your teacher. You are convinced that your teacher doesn't like you.

3. It is the third week of the semester, and you are in an English composition class that you need to pass as a requirement for graduation. The professor talks to you after class and tells you that your grammar problems are very serious and that you are going to have a difficult time passing the class.

4. It is the week before the beginning of school. One of your favorite professors suggested that you take a class she is teaching. When you try to register by phone, you hear that the class is full.

5. You are taking a class which requires that you use the university computer lab. Other students in the class already have an I.D. card that gives them entrance to the lab. You are considering dropping the class because you don't have the card. Also, you don't feel comfortable using the computers that are in the lab.

6. On the first day of class, your professor gives the students her e-mail address and says that e-mail communication will be encouraged throughout the semester. You've never used e-mail before, and you didn't understand the instructions on how to use it.

7. After the first week of school, it seems that you are taking too many classes and that you won't be able to handle all of the work. You feel overloaded, and you're not sure what to do because you think that you need all of the classes.

REAL PEOPLE/REAL VOICES

LANGUAGE LEARNING STRATEGY

Increase your listening comprehension by predicting the language you will hear in a specific situation. Before you go into a situation, try to make predictions about vocabulary, expressions, and what people will say in that situation. Picture the situation in your mind and try to see the speakers who will be using the language. Then predict the words and expressions that you will hear in the situation, and make a list of these. Finally, predict the statements or questions you will hear in the situation, and make a list of these.

Apply the Strategy

You are going to hear two students, Alex and Sheva, discussing the beginning of the semester at college. They will talk about why the beginning of the semester is frustrating and confusing. They will also discuss the strategies they use to overcome the obstacles they face. Make predictions about the language you will hear in this situation by following the directions below.

Getting Ready to Listen

1. Take the following steps so that you can picture the situation in your mind:

   a. Alex and Sheva are college students. Make predictions about the appearance of college students.

   b. Describe what their college campus might look like.

   c. Describe what their classroom might look like.

2. Write five words you expect to hear in the conversation:

   _____   _____

   _____   _____

   _____

3. Predict three statements or questions you will hear during the conversation.

_____

_____

_____

 Listen

Listening 2: Alex's and Sheva's Experiences

1. As you listen to the tape the first time, check the statements that you hear in the conversation.

   a. _____ If I want to add a class, I get there early for the teacher's signature.

   b. _____ I don't like teachers who give a lot of homework.

   c. _____ The first day of class is important because you find out about the work for the semester.

   d. _____ It's really important to study hard for exams.

   e. _____ I always look at the books in the bookstore to get a good idea about the class.

   f. _____ I get really frustrated if I can't add a class that I need.

2. As you listen to the tape a second time, write down three obstacles Alex and Sheva face. For each obstacle, write down the strategy they use to deal with the obstacle.

OBSTACLES	STRATEGIES
1. _____ _____	1. _____ _____
2. _____ _____	2. _____ _____
3. _____ _____	3. _____ _____

After You Listen

After you listen to the tape, discuss the following questions with a partner.

1. Look at the list of words that you predicted in "Getting Ready to Listen." Did you hear any of the words as you listened to the tape?

2. Have you ever experienced any of the frustration that Alex and Sheva described? How did you handle it? Have you ever used any of their strategies?

3. What are some additional frustrations or obstacles that you have experienced as you've begun school? What strategies did you use to deal with them?

The Sound of It: Pronunciation of Prepositions

Listen to the tape again. As you hear each of the following phrases, notice how they are pronounced. The prepositions are not pronounced as they are written. Write them in a way that represents how they are pronounced.

EXAMPLE: **beginning of the semester** *beginning uh the semester*

1. **kind of** _____

2. **try to prepare** _____

3. **go to the** _____

4. **look at them** _____

5. **for the semester** _____

6. **or drop it** _____

7. **taken care of all** _____

PART 2: Understanding a Teacher's Objectives and Expectations

Getting Ready to Read

You are going to read an excerpt from "Everybody Else's College Education" by Louis Menand. In this article, he discusses some of the changes that have occurred in college education.

Below is a list of words and phrases that appear in the article. The vocabulary is related to higher education. Write a definition for each of the vocabulary items. If you're not sure of the meaning, make a guess.

1. student body: _____

_____

2. undergraduates: _____

_____

3. field of study: _____

_____

4. specialize: _____

_____

5. basic skills: _____

_____

6. vocational preparation: _____

_____

7. scholarly pursuits: _____

_____

Read

As you read, underline any changes that have occurred in college education.

1   . . . Student bodies are not only more diverse in terms of ethnicity, income and age; they are also more heterogeneous in terms of preparation and aptitude. Today's students do not all have the same interests, nor do they wish to learn the same things. In the

typical college classroom, the social, cultural and intellectual differences among individual students are immediately and persistently in evidence.

2   So are the differences in need and expectation. In the conventional picture, undergraduates specialize in a field of study—physics or philosophy or French—which they learn by listening to lectures and reading books. When they graduate, at 21 or 22, they have plenty of time to consider their career options or to return for advanced study. In reality, many students now come to college later in life, are less prepared to undertake academic inquiry and have less leisure for scholarly pursuits. Their interest in education is likely to be far more practical than that of the student of 30 years ago, for whom merely having attended college was a cashable distinction. Students these days may need work on basic skills—for many, English is a second language—and they may regard college as vocational preparation in a much-less-abstract sense than students once did. . . .

◆**After You Read**

Make a list of the changes from the conventional portrait of college education and the one that Menand is describing in the present.

1. _____
2. _____
3. _____
4. _____
5. _____

Now look at each of the changes you listed from the reading. Do you know about any similarities to the direction of higher education in your native culture?

THE FIRST DAY OF CLASS

When you begin a new semester, you may be taking a number of classes taught by different teachers. The first day of class is very important because that's when you find out about the objectives for the class. You also find out what is required of you. Every teacher is different. You will feel less overwhelmed if you are able to understand the objectives a particular teacher has for the class. It will also help to understand the expectations the teacher has for the students in the class. When you understand these things, you can prepare yourself. You can find ways to work towards the objectives and fulfill the expectations of the teacher.

Below are statements that a teacher could make on the first day of class. For each statement, work with a partner to complete the following tasks:

(a) Paraphrase what the teacher is saying.

(b) Summarize what the teacher expects of you.

EXAMPLE: "I will accept no late assignments."

(a) Paraphrase: "The teacher is saying that students must turn in homework on the due date, and cannot turn it in late."

(b) Summarize: "I have to be very careful about assignment deadlines and be sure to manage my time so that I can turn in assignments on time."

1. "My office hours are Monday through Friday 10–11 a.m., but if you need to see me at a different time, just let me know."

   Paraphrase: _____

   _____

   Summarize: _____

   _____

2. "If I catch anyone plagiarizing a term paper, it's an automatic failure."

   Paraphrase: _____

   _____

   Summarize: _____

   _____

3. "On the syllabus, you will find reading assignments, due dates for term papers, and exam dates."

   Paraphrase: _____

   _____

   Summarize: _____

   _____

4. "If your language skills are below level, you will not pass this class."

   Paraphrase: _____

   _____

   Summarize: _____

   _____

   _____

5. "I don't care if you can recite facts and dates. I want to see that you're thinking critically."

   Paraphrase: _____

   _____

   Summarize: _____

   _____

   _____

6. "If you have any questions, you can e-mail me, and you can also go to the web site to find additional exercises and extra-credit assignments for class."

   Paraphrase: _____

   _____

   Summarize: _____

   _____

   _____

7. "This class requires that you do a lot of difficult reading and participate actively in class to discuss the reading. It's through the discussion that we can really discover the deeper meanings of the literature."

   Paraphrase: _____

   _____

   Summarize: _____

   _____

   _____

THE INTRODUCTORY LECTURE

LANGUAGE LEARNING STRATEGY

Learn to identify the parts of a lecture as you're listening. It will help you organize the information, take notes, and increase your comprehension. In order to identify the parts of a lecture, listen for key words, such as *first of all, before I discuss that . . ., the most important thing to remember is . . ., so . . ., finally . . ., now that you understand . . ., remember. . . .* Also, if you know the topic, predict how the lecture will be divided into the *beginning,* the *middle,* and the *end.* The beginning usually introduces the subject and gives background information. The middle focuses on the main idea of the lecture and gives important facts and details. The end summarizes the main points and emphasizes the most important ideas. Using these techniques, listen to the lecture and divide your notes into parts.

Apply the Strategy

You are going to hear a lecture given by a professor on the first day of an advanced reading and composition class. Complete the activities below to practice identifying the parts of a lecture.

◀Getting Ready to Listen

Predict what the parts of the lecture might be. Discuss your predictions with a partner; then write them below.

Beginning: What do you think the subject will be, and what background information do you think the professor will give?

_____

_____

_____

Middle: What do you think the main idea of the lecture might be? What facts and details do you think the professor will be giving?

_____

_____

_____

End: What important ideas do you think the professor will emphasize at the end?

_____

_____

_____

 Listen

Listening 3: The Introductory Lecture

As you listen to the lecture, write down any key words that identify
the parts of the lecture.

_____   _____

_____   _____

_____   _____

_____   _____

As you listen to the lecture a second time, write **B** if the idea comes
at the beginning of the lecture, write **M** if the idea comes in the middle of the lecture, and write **E** if the idea comes at the end of the
lecture.

1. _____ In writing, we will be working on your paraphrasing,
   summarizing, and essay-writing skills.

2. _____ If you work hard and really participate in class, you will
   make progress and enjoy the class.

3. _____ The standards for this class are quite high.

4. _____ We're going to be reading quite a variety of stories, articles, and essays, and you'll have frequent opportunities
   to write.

5. _____ We will have regular in-class graded assignments, and
   you will turn in a portfolio of your work at the end of the
   semester.

6. _____ Let's talk about some of the objectives and requirements
   for the class.

7. _____ I'm going to talk a bit about this level and what it means
   to be in English 400.

8. _____ Our goal is to improve reading and writing skills.

9. _____ This class is the last class in the sequence before you're
   eligible for the composition class.

> **45 U.S. universities
> have an acceptance
> rate of 100%.**
>
> **—NELSON AND PREZIOSI**

◆ **After You Listen**

Review the predictions you made in "Getting Ready to Listen." Did you accurately predict the parts of the lecture?

Culture Note

Generally, in the United States grades are used to evaluate a student's progress. However, some people disagree with this method of evaluation. Sometimes other methods of evaluation are used. Teachers may have a system of grading that gives the student more responsibility. For example, a student may sign a contract for a grade at the beginning of the class. The student has to fulfill the requirements agreed to in the contract in order to receive a specific grade. What is the system of grading in your native culture? What kinds of grades are used? How important are grades to a student's future? Do you agree with the grading system? Find out about the grading system used in the culture of another student in your class. Compare it to the grading system in your native culture. Discuss how you feel about grades as a method of evaluation.

DEBATE

. . . .

Part 1

Education in the United States stresses the importance of critical thinking. At the college level, teachers expect students to be able to think critically, not only recite facts and details. Here are some questions to keep in mind when you are asked to think critically about something. If you pay attention to these questions, you will be able to develop your critical thinking skills.

a. **What does the text really mean?**

   Try to go beneath the surface to discover the deeper meaning of what you read or what someone is saying.

b. **What is the value of the opposite point of view? (This is called "playing the devil's advocate.")**

Explore the opposite point of view so that you fully understand it. That will deepen understanding of your point of view as well.

c. **What distinctions can be made between the ideas in A and B?**

See the distinctions between things so that you can have a clear picture of the separate issues.

d. **What are the important details?**

Cut through the generalizations to specific information that clarifies the issue.

There are different opinions about using grades to evaluate academic progress. Some people think that giving grades is not a good way to motivate students to learn or to evaluate their progress. You will have a debate about grading. You will argue either for or against grades. Read each of the following opinions for and against grades and think about the position you would like to take. Keep in mind the questions that develop your critical thinking skills.

Against Grades

1. "Grades shouldn't be used as the motivation to learn."

2. "It's impossible for teachers to grade objectively. Usually grades are based on very subjective conditions like personality and appearance of the student."

For Grades

1. "Grades are the only systematic way to evaluate student progress and are therefore necessary."

2. "Students expect to get feedback from teachers, so they should receive grades for their work."

Part 2

Now decide which side you would like to debate—for or against grades. With the other students who share your opinion, discuss at least two arguments for your position. For each argument, write two statements which support that argument.

Argument 1: _____

_____

_____

Supporting Statement: _____

_____

_____

Supporting Statement: _____

_____

_____

Argument 2: _____

_____

_____

Supporting Statement: _____

_____

_____

Supporting Statement: _____

_____

_____

Part 3

Once you have prepared your arguments, take turns with other members of your group to present your arguments to the other side. Use your arguments and supporting statements during the debate.

Write About It.

Think about a teacher you've had at any time in your life who has had a great influence on you. Why did the teacher influence you so strongly? What characteristics did the teacher have that made him or her special? Write about this teacher on the lines below.

_____

_____

_____

_____

_____

_____

_____

_____

"GOOD" TEACHER . . . "BAD" TEACHER

What makes a "good" teacher? What makes a "bad" teacher? Think about your experiences in school and other situations in which you have had teachers. In a small group, make a list of characteristics, requirements, and conditions that make a "good" teacher. Make a list of characteristics that make a "bad" teacher. Use the new language from this chapter to ask about alternatives and state preferences.

EXAMPLE: I would much rather have a strict teacher that I can learn from than an easy teacher.

Good Teacher	Bad Teacher

TUNING IN: "Freshmen Fears"

You are going to watch a video about a student starting as a freshman (first year student) at a large university in the United States. Before you watch the video, discuss the following questions:

1. What do you think freshmen might be afraid of? Write down two fears you think they might have.

   _____

   _____

   _____

   _____

2. What do you think the parents of freshmen might be afraid of? Write down two fears you think they might have.

   _____

   _____

   _____

   _____

UCLA had 29,302 applicants in 1998, more than any other U.S. university.

—NELSON AND PREZIOSI

© CNN

As you watch the video, write **T** if the statement is true and **F** if the statement is false.

1. _____ Debbie Parks is worried about her son James starting school.

2. _____ James is worried about getting lost.

3. _____ There are fewer than 27,000 students at North Carolina State.

4. _____ Freshmen feel overwhelmed by the size of the school.

5. _____ Ten to fifteen percent of freshmen drop out of college.

Discussion

Imagine that you are James starting as a freshman at North Carolina State. What would you like to be included in your orientation to the university?

PUTTING IT ALL TOGETHER

1. List two ways that the beginning of school can cause confusion or frustration.

   _____

   _____

   _____

   _____

2. List two ways that you can overcome obstacles at the beginning of school.

   _____

   _____

   _____

   _____

3. Complete the following statements with expressions used to ask about alternatives:

   a. _____ take the placement test on Friday,

   _____ to take it another day?

   b. _____ teachers who offer this class?

4. Complete the following statements with expressions used to state preferences:

   a. _____ buy my books early _____

   _____ I can avoid the lines.

   b. _____ take a science class this semester

   _____ take other classes that require a

   _____ higher level of English.

5. List five words that you would expect to hear a teacher say in a lecture about the syllabus and course requirements on the first day of class.

   _____   _____

   _____   _____

   _____

Test-Taking Tip

Work with a partner to prepare for speaking-based tests. Practice speaking with your partner about subjects you think you may be asked about on the test. First, one of you can play the part of the "interviewer" while the other takes the role of the "interviewee;" then you can reverse roles. The interviewer should prepare questions to ask before the practice interview begins.

CHECK YOUR PROGRESS

On a scale of 1 to 5, where 1 means "not at all," 2 means "not very well," 3 means "moderately well," 4 means "well," and 5 means "very well," rate how well you have mastered the goals set at the beginning of the chapter:

1 2 3 4 5   overcome confusion and frustration at the beginning of school.

1 2 3 4 5   communicate about academic procedures and requirements.

1 2 3 4 5   increase listening comprehension by predicting the language in a specific situation.

1 2 3 4 5   ask about alternatives and state preferences.

1 2 3 4 5   learn to identify the parts of a lecture while listening.

1 2 3 4 5   understand teachers' objectives and expectations.

If you've given yourself a 3 or lower on any of these goals:

- visit the *Tapestry* web site for additional practice.
- ask your instructor for extra help.
- review the sections of the chapter that you found difficult.
- work with a partner or study group to further your progress.

Very often it's possible to increase your potential to learn and understand by guessing meaning. You may feel uncomfortable guessing because this means you are not certain of the answer. In this chapter, we will discuss differences between people and cultures. With this in mind, look at the title of this chapter. Guess what the Native Americans meant when they used the complete saying, which is "You never understand people until you've walked a mile in their moccasins."

2

WALKING A MILE IN ANOTHER PERSON'S MOCCASINS— CROSS-CULTURAL COMMUNICATION

Learning to express yourself clearly in a second language can be challenging. A lot of time is spent studying grammar, vocabulary, idioms and slang, and all the other parts of the language. However, there is one challenge that is often almost forgotten—the challenge of culture. Culture influences how language is used appropriately in different situations. In our increasingly global community, learning a language is not enough anymore. It is also necessary to understand the culture that gave birth to that particular language. In addition to vocabulary and grammar, everyone needs lessons in patience and tolerance, too. The purpose of this chapter is to open up discussion of language and culture and to give you some speaking skills that will make it easier to handle cultural issues as they come up. These skills will also be useful to you throughout the text and throughout your education as you explore issues and ideas with your fellow students both inside and outside the classroom environment.

Setting Goals

In this chapter you will learn how to:

◈ use specific methods to communicate effectively with people from other cultures.

◈ use appropriate language to solve problems.

◈ recognize and use direct speech.

◈ recognize and use subtle speech.

◈ contribute your ideas in group activities.

◆ **Getting Started**

Complete the following statements. There are no right or wrong answers. The purpose of the activity is to examine your beliefs, attitudes, and feelings. It's very important to be aware of these things as you explore different cultures. After you have completed the statements by yourself, discuss your answers with a partner.

What Do I Know About the Topic?

1. The most important thing to do in order to communicate effectively with people from other countries is . . .

2. Communication involves language and . . .

3. I think people from all countries share the same values because . . . One example is . . .

4. One thing I worry about when I talk to a student or teacher from another culture is . . .

5. One thing I look forward to when I talk to a student or teacher from another culture is . . .

6. When I speak to people from other countries/cultures, I usually try to . . .

7. When I am in class and a student from another country takes a long time to answer a teacher's question, I think it means that he or she . . .

8. I would/would not interrupt another student in class because . . .

What Do I Know About the Language?

1. I know someone is being direct with me when they _____
   _____
   _____
   _____

2. If I want to say something that may hurt someone's feelings I ___
   _____
   _____
   _____

3. I think English is more/less direct than my native language because _____
   _____
   _____

PART 1: Experiencing Cultural Diversity in Ways That Problems Are Discussed

Discuss the following questions.

1. What is the ethnic makeup of your native country?

2. What kinds of problems can exist between people from different countries or cultures? How are these problems usually solved?

3. Have you ever had a disagreement or misunderstanding with someone from another culture? What happened?

LANGUAGE YOU CAN USE: DIRECT VS. SUBTLE SPEECH

It is clear that culture plays a big part in communicating effectively. Sometimes, people are rude without meaning to be. Sometimes, people do not communicate what they mean, even though they may be trying hard. Often, poor communication results from having different ideas about the correct way to say things—when to be very direct so people understand, and when to be less direct to be polite. Learning ways to be direct and ways to be indirect, or subtle, makes it possible to choose the best way to say things. Following are some different ways that people talk in the classroom about problems and solutions. Some of the language is direct. Some is not so direct; it is subtle. Look at the examples.

All cultures value honesty, but there are differences in how directly people say things.

SITUATION	DIRECT	SUBTLE
A native English-speaking student uses a lot of slang. The slang is not familiar. You don't understand.	"You should use words everyone understands."	"I'm not quite sure what that means."
A student in class feels that the class is not satisfying her needs. Perhaps the material is too easy, or the student is not sure what the purpose of the lesson is.	"This material is really boring." "I'm really unhappy in this class."	"I'm not sure I understand. . . . Would you mind explaining?" "I think I might learn more if. . . ."
The teacher of your class speaks very quickly. Often, it is difficult to understand what the teacher is saying.	"You talk too fast." "I can't understand anything you say."	"I'm sorry. I missed that. Could you repeat it?" "Would you mind slowing down a bit?"

Culture Note

In some cultures it is fine to be very direct with someone about what you are feeling and thinking. However, other cultures place a high value on *tact,* on being gentle and indirect in speech in order to protect the feelings of others. What is important in your native culture? Discuss this with other students in your class.

USING NEW LANGUAGE

Tolerance and cele-bration of individual differences is the fire that fuels lasting love.

—TOM HANNAH

Individually, look at the situations below, which could easily happen in an English-speaking country. Decide if you would respond directly or subtly in each situation, and think about why you would do this. Then use the language presented above to write down what you would say. Practice your response with a partner.

1. Your friend is wearing a new shirt. She asks you what you think of this shirt. You think it is rather unattractive.

   Would you respond directly or subtly? _____

   Why? _____

   What would you say? _____

2. You are talking to one of your teachers. During the conversation the teacher uses a word that you do not understand. You want the teacher to explain this word.

   Would you respond directly or subtly? _____

   Why? _____

   What would you say? _____

3. You are taking a test in class. Another student keeps trying to look at your test to see your answers. You do not want the student to look at your test. You are afraid the teacher will get angry.

   Would you respond directly or subtly? _____

   Why? _____

   What would you say? _____

4. You are driving some friends to a party. One of your friends asks if you would mind stopping to pick up yet another person. You are in a hurry; besides, you do not like the person your friend wants you to pick up.

   Would you respond directly or subtly? _____

   Why? _____

   What would you say? _____

5. Your teacher has finished explaining the homework to the class. The explanation was not clear, and many students are confused about what they are supposed to do.

   Would you respond directly or subtly? _____

   Why? _____

   What would you say? _____

Culture Note

In some cultures, it is OK to share information and work together on tests. In many countries, including the United States, the teacher often expects students to take tests without any help from other students. Working together is not allowed. When students work together, even though they have been told not to, this is called *cheating*. Do you think it is cheating if students work together?

LISTEN FOR THE LANGUAGE

LANGUAGE LEARNING STRATEGY

Learn the difference between polite speech and rude speech. This will help you say the right thing in the right way. It can be very difficult to speak in English. You have to worry about vocabulary and grammar, and you probably also worry about being polite. Usually, the more polite you want to be, the more indirectly you will say something. Very direct speech is often considered rude, unless you know the other person very well.

Apply the Strategy

In the next activity, listen carefully to what the people say. Listen for polite speech. Decide if the people are being direct or indirect. Why do they speak this way?

Getting Ready to Listen

In a few minutes you will hear a conversation between two people. Speaker A is talking about going out to dinner with Speaker B. Speaker B is not very interested. Below you will find one-half of the conversation. With a partner, complete the conversation. First, complete it using direct responses. Then complete it using subtle, indirect responses. If you need help with direct and subtle language, look back at the examples at the top of page 32. If you have time, practice the dialogues together when you finish them.

1. Use direct responses.

   Speaker A: Hey, I'm hungry. How about you? Did you eat yet?

   Speaker B: _____

   Speaker A: I was thinking about something ethnic. Do you like Thai food?

   Speaker B: _____

   Speaker A: Yeah, and I know a great place downtown. You ever been to Thai Heaven?

   Speaker B: _____

Speaker A: Yeah, the prices are really reasonable and the food's great—really authentic. How does that sound to you?

Speaker B: _____

Speaker A: OK, so do you want me to pick you up?

Speaker B: _____

Speaker A: It's no trouble at all. How does eight o'clock sound?

Speaker B: _____

Speaker A: OK. Great! See you then.

2. Use indirect, subtle responses.

Speaker A: Hey, I'm hungry. How about you? Did you eat yet?

Speaker B: _____

Speaker A: I was thinking about something ethnic. Do you like Thai food?

Speaker B: _____

Speaker A: Yeah, and I know a great place downtown. You ever been to Thai Heaven?

Speaker B: _____

Speaker A: Yeah, the prices are really reasonable and the food's great—really authentic. How does that sound to you?

Speaker B: _____

Speaker A: OK, so do you want me to pick you up?

Speaker B: _____

Speaker A: It's no trouble at all. How does eight o'clock sound?

Speaker B: _____

Speaker A: OK. Great! See you then.

 Listen   ### Listening 1: Listening for the Language

You will hear the conversation more than once. As you listen, write down everything Speaker B says on the tape.

Speaker A: Hey, I'm hungry. How about you? Did you eat yet?

Speaker B: _____

Speaker A: I was thinking about something ethnic. Do you like Thai food?

Speaker B: _____

Speaker A: Yeah, and I know a great place downtown. You ever been to Thai Heaven?

Speaker B: _____

Speaker A: Yeah, the prices are really reasonable and the food's great—really authentic. How does that sound to you?

Speaker B: _____

Speaker A: OK, so do you want me to pick you up?

Speaker B: _____

Speaker A: It's no trouble at all. How does eight o'clock sound?

Speaker B: _____

Speaker A: OK. Great! See you then.

After You Listen

Answer the questions about the conversation on the tape.

1. On the tape, did Speaker B respond directly or subtly?

2. Do you think the responses were more direct or more subtle than the responses you and your partner wrote for your conversations?

3. Look at what you wrote down in "Listen." What language helped you to recognize direct or subtle speech? Copy those language cues below.

_____

_____

_____

_____

_____

_____

_____

The Sound of It: Reductions in Conversation

On the tape, Speaker A used several reductions. A reduction happens when words are run together. Native speakers use a lot of reductions in conversation. The words are not clear and separated.

Listen to the tape. You will hear the reductions. As you listen to the reductions, read along below. You will see the true speech and the reduced speech.

TRUE SPEECH	REDUCED SPEECH
1. Did you eat yet?	1. J'ya eetyet?
2. Do you like Thai food?	2. Ya like Thai food?
3. You ever been to Thai Heaven?	3. Y'ever been to Thai Heaven?
4. How does that sound to you?	4. Howzat sound to ya?
5. So, do you want me to pick you up?	5. So, d'ya want me to pick y'up?

PART 2: Participating in Cultural Diversity

Getting Ready to Read

Vocabulary Building

alienation	initial	sandwiched
anxiety	phenomena	symptoms
delight	resolution	withdrawal
identity		

Ten vocabulary words from the reading are listed above. Each word is used in a sentence below. Read the sentence; then choose the definition or synonym that you think matches the meaning of the **bold-faced** vocabulary word.

1. She felt that being a mother was the most important part of her **identity**, so it was hard when her children grew up and moved away.

   a) name   b) self-definition   c) personality

2. Coughing, sneezing, and a runny nose are **symptoms** of having a cold.

   a) illnesses   b) diseases   c) physical signs

3. If you drink too much coffee, the caffeine may cause **anxiety**.

   a) stress   b) anger   c) nervousness

4. Shy people often feel a sense of **withdrawal** when they are in very large groups.

   a) the desire to avoid others
   b) fear of people
   c) nervousness and discomfort

5. As a foreign student in a new country, everything was strange and uncomfortable at first. Anne experienced **alienation** for several weeks.

   a) sickness
   b) shyness
   c) feeling that one doesn't belong

6. Some people believe in ghosts. Others think this **phenomena** is not real.

   a) mystery
   b) something that can't be easily explained
   c) a surprise, something unexpected

7. The plane was very crowded. I was **sandwiched** between a big, tall man and a woman with a crying baby. It was an uncomfortable trip.

   a) squeezed   b) placed   c) sitting

8. When Tom got a ticket, his **initial** feeling was anger, but then he realized he really was driving too fast.

   a) first   b) later   c) last

9. When he won the lottery, he felt total **delight!** He smiled and smiled.

   a) shock   b) happiness, pleasure   c) surprise

10. He is firm in his **resolution** to eat less and exercise more.

   a) attempt   b) determination   c) promise

 Read

Handling Culture Shock

1 Somewhere along the line almost every ESL student who is far from home will experience a degree of culture shock—the situation in which the person's identity is challenged and various emotional and sometimes even physical symptoms begin to occur. . . . It can involve fear, anxiety, anger, depression, withdrawal, stress, alienation and illness, among other related phenomena.

> We hate some persons because we do not know them; and we will not know them because we hate them.
>
> —CHARLES CALEB COLTON

2   . . . We might say that culture shock occurs in several stages, which fall in the middle of the learner's experience. Culture-shock stages are sandwiched between the stage of initial delight felt by many travelers or visitors and the stage of deeper, more comfortable resolution. . . . What can be done about culture shock? Can it be prevented?

3   Culture shock cannot be prevented. . . . However, ESL teachers can cushion the blow somewhat. Sensitive teachers . . . allow their students the opportunity to discuss their feelings freely and to express any culture shock they may experience. Some of the best ways to open up the flow of communication about culture shock include literary opportunities, such as writing a poem or an essay for the class magazine, or role-playing activities in which the free expression of feelings is accepted.

After You Read

Answer the following questions about the reading. Rewrite ideas from the reading in your own words. Repeating something in your own words is a good way to remember it. This is called *paraphrasing*.

1. What is culture shock?

    _____
    _____
    _____

2. What are some feelings people may have during culture shock?

    _____
    _____
    _____

3. Is it possible to prevent culture shock?

    _____
    _____
    _____

4. What are some good ways to deal with culture shock?

    _____
    _____
    _____

Write About It.

In the space provided, respond to the questions below.

1. What is culture shock? Describe it in your own words.

_____

_____

_____

_____

2. What is an experience you have had with culture shock?

_____

_____

_____

_____

_____

REAL PEOPLE/REAL VOICES

On the tape you will hear two people speaking about their own experiences. Tamara is a woman from the United States who taught English in Korea. Kirk is a man from the United States who studied Spanish in Mexico.

Getting Ready to Listen

In this chapter you are learning about direct and indirect (subtle) speech. Kirk and Tamara will talk about this. Before you listen, fill in the blanks below. Use a scale of 1–5 (1 is indirect; 5 is very direct). Use your own knowledge, experiences, and some guesswork to rank each of the cultures below according to how direct you think they are.

_____ The United States   _____ Korea

_____ Mexico   _____ Your native culture

Listen

Listening 2: Tamara's and Kirk's Experiences

Read the statements on the next page. You will hear the tape more than once. As you listen, circle **True** if the statement is true. Circle **False** if the statement is false.

> Perhaps travel cannot prevent bigotry, but by demonstrating that all peoples cry, laugh, eat, worry, and die, it can introduce the idea that if we try and understand each other, we may even become friends.
>
> **—MAYA ANGELOU**

Tamara's Experience

1. True False   Tamara is an older woman.

2. True False   Tamara didn't know anything about Korea before she arrived there.

3. True False   Tamara is from California.

4. True False   Tamara's students felt comfortable asking her personal questions.

5. True False   Tamara felt comfortable answering direct questions about her personal life.

6. True False   Tamara understood why the students asked her these questions.

7. True False   Tamara continued to allow her students to ask her questions.

Kirk's Experience

1. True False   Kirk studied at several different schools in Mexico.

2. True False   Kirk's classes were large, with many students.

3. True False   Kirk thought his class in Mexico was more formal than a typical American class.

4. True False   Kirk was surprised at how directly students discussed certain topics in class.

5. True False   Kirk quickly felt comfortable making his own direct statements about difficult topics in class.

◀ After You Listen

Work with a partner. Respond to the questions below about what you heard on the tape. Answering these questions will help you understand and remember what you heard.

1. What kind of questions did Tamara's students ask her?

2. Do you think these questions are direct or subtle questions?

3. Would you feel comfortable answering these questions if a stranger asked you?

4. Would you feel comfortable answering these questions in front of a group of people?

5. What were some of the topics students discussed in Kirk's classes in Mexico?

6. Would you feel comfortable speaking openly and directly about these topics in a class?

7. What ratings did you give Korea and Mexico for directness in the "Getting Ready to Listen" section? Would you give these same ratings after listening to the tape?

8. What, if anything, surprised you as you listened to the tape?

9. After listening to the tape, do you think cultures and countries have the same ideas about what is direct and what is subtle?

10. Why is it important to realize that different cultures have different ideas and opinions about direct and subtle speech?

LANGUAGE LEARNING STRATEGY

Learn to communicate well with people from different cultures and backgrounds. This will help you feel comfortable and confident in class. Maybe you are in an ESL class with students from many countries. Maybe you are in a classroom with a lot of native English speakers and only a few non-native speakers. Improving your communication skills and learning to communicate without stereotypes will not only make you feel more comfortable; it will also help improve your learning.

Apply the Strategy

Use the ideas below to improve your cross-cultural communication:

1. Be aware of your own stereotypes about others.

2. Look for things you have in common with people who seem to be different. Maybe you all dislike having a lot of homework over the weekend.

3. Learn about other cultures. Observe. Ask questions.

4. Share ideas that teach people about your own culture.

Try to do these four things as you participate in the next activity.

Your next step is to experiment by experiencing some cultural problems for yourself. These problems show some of the small things that can make it hard to communicate, and can lead to culture shock. As you watch and participate, analyze what the specific problem is and how it can be resolved in a way that shows understanding of and respect for the various cultures involved. As you participate in this activity, try to be aware of what your partner is experiencing. This can make working with other people in class much more successful.

ROLE PLAYING

> The highest result of education is tolerance.
>
> —HELEN KELLER

You and another student will be asked to come to the front of the room. Your teacher will give you a piece of paper that describes your situation and gives you instructions. Your teacher will give you a few minutes to read the situation and prepare to act it out. When you're ready, act out the situation described in your instructions as closely as possible. As you watch and listen to other students acting out their simulations, work on the Situation Analysis Grid on the next page.*

As each pair is performing their simulation for the class, fill in the spaces in the first three columns. Follow the example provided, which analyzes Simulation 1. You will fill in the last three columns in small groups after the simulation activity is completed. Remember to remain neutral. Observe objectively. This makes it easier to find solutions.

Learning another language is not enough. More than words are necessary for successful communication across cultures.

*See pages 222–223 for Simulation Problems.

Simulation 1					
Problem A wants to look directly at B, but B doesn't like it.	**Reason** They have different ideas about direct eye contact.	**Perception** A thinks B is too shy, but B thinks A is very rude to stare at him/her.	Solution	Direct	Subtle

Simulation 2					
Problem	Reason	Perception	Solution	Direct	Subtle

Simulation 3					
Problem	Reason	Perception	Solution	Direct	Subtle

Simulation 4					
Problem	Reason	Perception	Solution	Direct	Subtle

Simulation 5					
Problem	Reason	Perception	Solution	Direct	Subtle

Simulation 5					
Problem	Reason	Perception	Solution	Direct	Subtle

ACADEMIC POWER STRATEGY

Contribute your ideas in group activities. Actively participating in group activities helps you remember your ideas and gives your teacher a chance to see you working hard to succeed in class. There are some easy things you can do to practice speaking in group discussions:

1. Ask questions. Ask your teacher. Ask other students. Show that you are interested and want to learn.

2. Use your notes to help prepare ideas you can share.

3. Paraphrase—repeat in your own words an idea from a lecture, discussion, or activity.

4. If you have something to say but it's not a good time, make a note to yourself and save your good idea to share later in the discussion.

Apply the Strategy

In small groups, discuss your observation of each simulation based on your notes in the grid. Be sure that everyone in the group contributes ideas. Compare your responses to other members of your group. Do you agree or disagree on the problem, the reason, and the perception?

TUNING IN: "The Bilingual Storyteller"

You will see a CNN video clip about a man who tries to help children be proud of their cultural identities. Before you watch the clip, talk with a partner and answer these questions.

Do you think it is easier for children or adults to adapt to a culture that is different from the culture of their families?

Why do you think this?

What are some of the things parents and other adults can do to help children become comfortable in a new culture?

© CNN

Antonio is a teacher. He tells stories to children. He tells the stories in a mix of English and Spanish. The stories help the children

> Let us not be blind to our differences—but let us also direct attention to our common interests and the means by which these differences can be resolved.
>
> **—JOHN F. KENNEDY**

feel comfortable living in a culture that is different from the culture of their families. You will see the video more than one time. As you watch the video, circle the correct answers to the questions below.

1. What English version of his name does Antonio use?

   a) Anthony   b) Tony

2. Antonio's father is Cuban. What nationality is his mother?

   a) Irish   b) Cuban

3. What is Antonio's job?

   a) teacher   b) actor

4. What does Antonio think immigrant children should do?

   a) try to be just like the people around them
   b) feel proud of their own culture and language

5. What do the children give Antonio at the end of the video?

   a) a sweatshirt with their handprints
   b) a photograph of the class

Do you have a story about your experiences? Find a partner. Tell him or her your story. Before telling the story, take some notes in the space below to help you remember and prepare to speak.

_____

_____

_____

_____

PUTTING IT ALL TOGETHER

1. List two behaviors you observed or discovered in this unit that are similar to your own culture.

   _____

   _____

2. List two behaviors you observed or learned about other cultures.

   _____

   _____

3. After finishing this chapter, what do you think is the most important thing to do in order to communicate effectively with people from other backgrounds?

_____

_____

_____

_____

4. List two or three strategies you can use the next time you feel uncomfortable with a person from another country.

_____

_____

_____

_____

A.

B.

5. Look at or take turns reading the conversations above and on the next page. The first line of the dialogue has been written for you. Write a subtle response and a direct response. Then explain to your classmates which response you would actually use, and why.

C. "I didn't study for the test. Do you mind if I look at your answers?"

D. "How do you like my new haircut?"

Test-Taking Tip

Pace yourself. Don't spend too much time on any single question. If you don't know the answer to a question, move on to the next question. Allow yourself some time near the end of the exam time to go back to the questions you skipped. Keep an eye on the time throughout the test.

CHECK YOUR PROGRESS

On a scale of 1 to 5, rate how well you have mastered the goals set at the beginning of the chapter:

1 2 3 4 5   use specific methods to communicate effectively with people from other cultures.

1 2 3 4 5   use appropriate language to solve problems.

1 2 3 4 5   recognize and use direct speech.

1 2 3 4 5   recognize and use subtle speech.

1 2 3 4 5   contribute your ideas in group activities.

If you've given yourself a 3 or lower on any of these goals:

- visit the *Tapestry* web site for additional practice.
- ask your instructor for extra help.
- review the sections of the chapter that you found difficult.
- work with a partner or study group to further your progress.

These photographs show different kinds of communication taking place between men and women. Because this communication is sometimes difficult, people say men and women are from different planets. Do you agree that it is difficult for men and women to understand each other because they are so different? What kind of experiences have you had trying to communicate with members of the opposite sex? Discuss this with your classmates.

3

I UNDERSTAND EXACTLY WHAT I THINK YOU SAID!

You have probably been involved in some kind of verbal conflict with a member of the opposite sex. Perhaps it was with a friend, family member, colleague, or someone with whom you were romantically involved. You are probably aware that effective communication is very important and not always easy. Words mean different things to different people, and often just listening to someone's words doesn't mean you truly understand what he or she is saying and feeling. In this chapter, you will examine how men and women communicate. You will practice some of the language that can be used to improve communication and resolve conflict. As you do the activities, think about the lessons you learned about communication in Chapter Two and apply what you learned.

Setting Goals

In this chapter you will learn how to:

◈ plan in advance in order to get the most out of each class session.

◈ take notes as you observe and listen to a conversation.

◈ ask for clarification.

◈ give clarification of your point of view.

◈ paraphrase what someone communicates to you.

◈ communicate more effectively with members of the opposite sex.

◈ express empathy for another person's feelings.

 **Getting Started**

What Do I Think About the Topic?

Answer the questions below to examine some of your thoughts about the topic of this chapter.

1. Do you think men and women have distinct ways of communicating?

    _____ Yes   _____ No

If you answered "Yes," what words would you use to describe the way they communicate?

EXAMPLE: sincere

Men: _____

Women: _____

2. On a scale of 1 to 5, rate your ability to communicate with members of the opposite sex.

1	2	3	4	5
poor				excellent

3. Do you think it is possible for men and women to learn how to communicate better with each other?

    _____ Yes   _____ No

What Do I Know About the Language?

1. Check the responses listed below that you use most often when you don't understand what someone is saying.

    _____ pretend I understand

    _____ ask questions

    _____ change the subject

    _____ feel embarrassed

    _____ blame the other person

    _____ restate what was said in my own words

    _____ ask for repetition

    _____ look words up in the dictionary

2. Which of the above responses would be most helpful for you to learn?

ACADEMIC POWER STRATEGY

Plan in advance in order to get the most out of each class session. If you plan in this way, you will be better prepared and you will learn more from a class. Before a class session, think about ways that you can get the most out of the class. For example, if you are in a class that requires a lot of discussion with your classmates, you can plan to be active during the discussion. Your plan will be most effective if you put it into writing or discuss it with a classmate. Follow these steps when you make your plan:

1. State two ways you plan to participate actively. (Examples: "I will ask more questions." "I will be a group leader." "I will express my opinion.")

2. State one question you have about the topic of the class. (Example: "Do women communicate differently in different cultures?")

3. State one problem that you would like to overcome. (Examples: "I would like to stop daydreaming during discussions." "I would like to be less shy.")

Apply the Strategy

Before you continue in this chapter, make a plan to get the most out of your next class session. Review the introduction to this chapter and think about the topic of the chapter. Complete the plan below to prepare yourself for the next class session.

My Plan for the Next Class Session

Step One. Two ways I can participate more actively:

1. _____

_____

2. _____

_____

Step Two. One question I have about the topic of the class:

_____

_____

Step Three. One problem I would like to overcome:

_____

_____

PART 1: "What Did You Say? What Did I Say?"

You have seen how the impact of culture can influence the way you communicate with other people. You have learned that something may be understood in one culture but may not be understood at all in another. It can be difficult to realize this because you begin your cultural learning at a very early age, and by the time you are an adult you have already formed set ideas about how to behave. Some psychologists and sociologists are taking this idea of cultural learning one step further. They believe that boys and girls learn different lessons about how to behave beginning when they are very young children. Then, when they become adults, they have communication problems just like two people who come from different cultures!

LANGUAGE LEARNING STRATEGY

Take notes as you observe and listen to a conversation, and you will increase your comprehension. Focus your attention on what you see and hear during the conversation by taking notes. Notice nonverbal clues such as facial expressions and gestures, which add to the meaning. This will help you to understand the communication more clearly. Follow these steps to take notes as you observe:

1. Focus on specific information in the conversation rather than trying to understand everything at once.

2. Write down the specific information that you are focusing on.

3. Observe nonverbal clues that show the feeling of the speakers.

4. Write down the nonverbal clues and the feelings they show.

Apply the Strategy

In the scenario activity that follows, take notes as you observe the scenarios. Follow the steps given in the "Language Learning Strategy."

SCENARIO ACTIVITY

Relationship =
connection =
union = link

Your teacher will give you a brief description of your part in a situation involving communication between two people. Read your description and act out the situation with your partner. Try to be as realistic as possible. You will not see what your partner's role in the situation is. As you watch other pairs act out the following scenarios, take notes about what the two partners are saying to each other. Notice how nonverbal clues help you understand how each person is feeling.*

Notes

Scenario 1: "The Husband, the Wife, and the Dream House"
What are they saying to each other?

Man: _____

Woman: _____

What nonverbal clues do you observe that show their feelings?

Nonverbal Clue   Feeling

_____   _____

_____   _____

Scenario 2: "The Colleague and the Computer"
What are they saying to each other?

Man: _____

Woman: _____

What nonverbal clues do you observe that show their feelings?

Nonverbal Clue   Feeling

_____   _____

_____   _____

Scenario 3: "The Wife's Night Out"
What are they saying to each other?

Man: _____

Woman: _____

*See pages 223–224 for scenario descriptions.

What nonverbal clues do you observe that show their feelings?

Nonverbal Clue   Feeling

_____   _____

_____   _____

Scenario 4: "Crying Over Coffee"

What are they saying to each other?

Man: _____

Woman: _____

What nonverbal clues do you observe that show their feelings?

Nonverbal Clue   Feeling

_____   _____

_____   _____

Scenario 5: "Getting Lost"

What are they saying to each other?

Man: _____

Woman: _____

What nonverbal clues do you observe that show their feelings?

Nonverbal Clue   Feeling

_____   _____

_____   _____

Scenario 6: "Improving Sales"

What are they saying to each other?

Man: _____

Woman: _____

What nonverbal clues do you observe that show their feelings?

Nonverbal Clue   Feeling

_____   _____

_____   _____

Discussion of Scenarios

Discuss each scenario that you saw, and refer to your notes to answer the following questions.

> Silence is one great art of conversation.
>
> **—ANONYMOUS**

1. What was each person trying to communicate to his or her partner? What response did each person expect?

2. How did the other person respond? How did that make the partner feel?

3. Why did each person respond in the way that they did?

4. How could each person have communicated differently to avoid a misunderstanding (if there was one)?

5. What stereotypes of men and women can you notice from these situations?

LANGUAGE YOU CAN USE: IMPROVING COMMUNICATION

The expressions below are useful for improving communication between men and women in relationships.

EXAMPLE 1

"I know it's my turn to cook, and I was wondering if you're really hungry."

Asking for Clarification	**"What exactly are you getting at?"**
Giving Clarification	"Well, what I mean is I haven't played tennis at all this week, and if I cook now, it will be too late to play."
Expressing Empathy	"I'm sorry that you haven't gotten to play tennis. I understand how much you enjoy it, but I'm really hungry now, so how about if we just have dinner separately tonight?"

Empathy/empathize = identify with = put oneself into another's shoes (remember walking a mile in another person's moccasins?)

EXAMPLE 2

"I need some space in our relationship."

Asking for Clarification	**"So, what you really mean is** you don't want to see me anymore?"
Giving Clarification	"No, **what I'm trying to say is** I do think we've been spending too much time together."
Expressing Empathy	**"I understand how you can feel that way.** We've seen each other every night this week."

USING NEW LANGUAGE

Review your notes on the scenarios from the previous activity. Choose two of the scenarios and work with a partner to write a dialogue for each scenario. In your dialogue, apply the skills of asking for clarification, giving clarification, and expressing empathy to avoid the misunderstanding that applied to the scenario. Refer to the example below to help you get started.

Scenario 1: The Husband, the Wife, and the Dream House

Wife: Wouldn't it be nice to have a bigger house, someday?
Husband: *What are you getting at?* Do you want to buy a new house soon? I don't really think we can afford it right now.
Wife: I know we can't afford it, but I enjoy thinking about our future together and planning things we can look forward to.
Husband: *I understand how you can feel that way.* Sometimes I like to think about the things we'll finally have time to do when we retire.

Scenario # _____

Speaker A: _____

Speaker B: _____

Speaker A: _____

Speaker B: _____

Speaker A: _____

Speaker B: _____

Scenario # _____

Speaker A: _____

Speaker B: _____

Speaker A: _____

Speaker B: _____

Speaker A: _____

Speaker B: _____

TUNING IN: "Anti-Divorce Class"

You are going to see a video about a workshop designed to prevent divorce. Before you watch the video, think about some common problems that can cause couples to divorce. Discuss this with a partner and list three problems below.

© CNN

1. _____

_____

_____

2. _____

_____

_____

3. _____

_____

_____

As you watch the video the first time, write **T** if the statement is true. Write **F** if the statement is false.

1. _____ 30% of all Americans get divorced.

2. _____ 50% of the marriages in Cobb County, Georgia, end in divorce.

3. _____ The method used in the workshop is role playing.

4. _____ The workshop costs $150.

5. _____ Couples take the workshop because of the reality that marriage can go wrong.

As you watch the video a second time, complete the following notes. In the workshop, couples receive counseling on how to deal with:

1. _____

2. _____

3. _____

Common problems that can destroy a marriage are:

1. _____

2. _____

3. _____

Compare the list of problems you discussed before you watched the video with the problems that were mentioned in the video. Were they similar? Discuss a specific situation that a couple could role play for one of these problems. For example, in the video one of the couples was role playing a discussion about sharing the housework.

The Sound of It: Syllable Stress

Below are some of the words that were used in the video. Listen to the video one more time and place a stress marker (´) on the syllable that receives the strongest stress.

1. romance   6. conduct

2. expectations   7. stubbornness

3. reality   8. exercises

4. divorce   9. prospects

5. marriage   10. future

PART 2: Who Said That?

In this part of the chapter you will continue to explore the ways that communication between the genders can be difficult. Often these misunderstandings can happen because we have certain expectations about each gender. For example, we expect men and women to have specific characteristics that affect how they communicate with each other. These are called *gender stereotypes*. You will have a chance to discover what your gender stereotypes are and how they may affect communication between men and women.

BRAINSTORMING: "MEN/WOMEN ARE SO . . .!"

In small groups, take a few minutes to share ideas about what characteristics you think are stereotypical of men and what characteristics you think are stereotypical of women. It's important to examine these stereotypes and ask ourselves whether they are accurate just as we do with stereotypes about people from other cultures. Here are two sample stereotypes to help you get started:

MEN	WOMEN
Men are *logical*.	Women are *emotional*.
_____	_____
_____	_____
_____	_____
_____	_____
_____	_____
_____	_____

True or False?

Read each of the following statements and discuss with your classmates what the statement means. Then discuss whether the statement is true or false and where these stereotypes may have come from. Do they correspond to the stereotypes you came up with in the brainstorming activity? How do you think these stereotypes may influence communication between men and women?

> In the Roman empire, marriage was not a legal formality; a man and a woman simply began to live together in a permanent household.
>
> —*AMERICAN ACADEMIC ENCYCLOPEDIA*

1. _____ Men equate sex with self-esteem.
2. _____ Women equate attractiveness with self-esteem.
3. _____ Men can't accept criticism from women.
4. _____ Women cry when they are criticized.
5. _____ Little boys are taught not to feel.
6. _____ Little girls are taught that feelings are OK.
7. _____ Men are competitive.
8. _____ Women are not competitive.
9. _____ Men are not sensitive to the feelings of others.
10. _____ Women are too emotional and sensitive.

LANGUAGE LEARNING STRATEGY

Paraphrase orally to help communicate meaning accurately and avoid translation into your native language. When you are able to paraphrase in a second language, you express the meaning in your own words. As your paraphrasing skills develop, you don't need to translate into your native language in order to understand the meaning and express it well. Follow these steps for paraphrasing orally:

1. Repeat orally the original text you want to paraphrase so that you "hear" it and understand it.
2. Make changes to the original text by doing any of the following:
   * find synonyms for the words or expressions in the original text
   * find antonyms for the words or expressions in the original text

- change word forms, e.g. adjectives to verbs
- change the word order

3. Communicate the meaning of the original text in your own words, using the changes you made.

Apply the Strategy

Use the steps for developing your paraphrasing skills as you complete the guessing activity below.

GUESSING ACTIVITY

In Chapter Two you made guesses about the meaning of a saying. Now you are going to use your beliefs about men and women as well as beliefs you have heard expressed by others, and you are going to make guesses about some quotations. (1) Read each of the quotations below. (2) Discuss the meaning with a partner. (3) Paraphrase the quotation so that you're expressing the original meaning in your own words. (4) Decide what stereotypes about men and women are being expressed by the quotation. (5) Discuss whether you agree or disagree with the views being expressed.

1. Quotation: "In our civilization, men are afraid that they will not be men enough, and women are afraid they might be considered only women." (Theidor Reik)

   Paraphrase: _____

   Stereotype: _____

   Do You Agree or Disagree? _____

   Why? _____

   _____

2. Quotation: "A woman's guess is much more accurate than a man's certainty." (Rudyard Kipling)

   Paraphrase: _____

   Stereotype: _____

   Do You Agree or Disagree? _____

   Why? _____

   _____

3. Quotation: "Women are not men's equals in anything except responsibility. We are not their inferiors either, or even
their superiors. We are quite simply different races." (Phyllis
McGinley)

Paraphrase: _____

Stereotype: _____

Do You Agree or Disagree? _____

Why? _____

_____

4. Quotation: "Women like silent men—they think they're listening."
(Marcel Achard)

Paraphrase: _____

Stereotype: _____

Do You Agree or Disagree? _____

Why? _____

_____

5. Quotation: "Man's love is of man's life a thing apart, it's woman's
whole existence." (Lord Byron)

Paraphrase: _____

Stereotype: _____

Do You Agree or Disagree? _____

Why? _____

_____

6. Quotation: "Women speak because they wish to speak, whereas
a man speaks only when driven to speech by something outside
himself—like for instance, he can't find any clean socks." (Jean
Kerr)

Paraphrase: _____

Stereotype: _____

Do You Agree or Disagree? _____

Why? _____

_____

The gender stereotypes you have been discussing are very strong in traditional cultures. If you think about your native culture, you may find that some of these stereotypes are still very strong although they may have changed somewhat in the past twenty years. In the United States and Canada, men and women have become more sensitive to these stereotypes, especially in cases where they lead to misunderstanding and discrimination. During the feminist revolution in the 1960s, women fought to break down some of these stereotypes to prevent these kinds of problems. However, the problems have not disappeared. Today there are laws created to protect men and women against harmful effects of gender stereotyping. For example, there are sexual harassment laws that deal with the way men and women behave and talk to each other in the workplace. Do you know about any such laws in your native culture?

◆ Getting Ready to Read

Vocabulary Building

Before you read, become familiar with the new vocabulary. For each word or expression from the reading, you will find an example of the vocabulary used in another context. Try to guess the meaning of the word from the context.

1. save face _____

   Context: After the president was accused of having an affair, he tried to **save face** by apologizing.

   Meaning: _____

2. self-deprecating

   Context: Chen made **self-deprecating** remarks during the interview to avoid appearing proud.

   Meaning: _____

3. self-effacing

   Context: Her **self-effacing** remarks made the director think that she was unqualified.

   Meaning: _____

4. couch

   Context: The teacher tried to **couch** her criticism of the student by praising him first.

   Meaning: _____

5. subordinate

   Context: It is difficult for a **subordinate** to criticize her manager.

   Meaning: _____

6. backfire

   Context: Lying to your wife could **backfire** by making her more suspicious and mistrustful of you.

   Meaning: _____

7. preface

   Context: It is advisable to **preface** a criticism with a positive comment to undercut the negative feelings that may arise.

   Meaning: _____

8. misinterpreted

   Context: Rebecca **misinterpreted** her boyfriend's serious tone as a sign of anger.

   Meaning: _____

 Read

You are going to read part of an interview with Deborah Tannen, a sociolinguist who has researched and written about communication between the genders. In this part of the interview, she is discussing the communication styles she wrote about in her book *You Just Don't Understand*. She is explaining how these communication styles affect men and women when they're working together. As you read, think about the following questions:

1. What is the communication style of women in the workplace?

2. In what way is the workplace still conducted by the "boys' rules"?

Gender Games

1 **Are the male and female communication styles described in *You Just Don't Understand* evident at work?**

2   Yes, they are. Women often use indirect, self-deprecating language and couch things in a way that allows the other person to save face, which can be easily misinterpreted by men. For example, a woman running a meeting might say to a subordinate who comes unprepared, "I'm sorry I didn't remind you that issue was

coming up today." She expects him to say, "I really should have known. You told me about the meeting." But instead he may be silent and think, "If she wants to take the blame, let her."

3 **What are the consequences of this for working women?**

4   A self-effacing style can backfire in the workplace because it appears to undercut a woman's authority. Almost every woman I know has had the experience of saying something in a meeting and being ignored. Then a man says essentially the same thing, and everybody picks up on it as a great idea. Sometimes a woman will preface her remark by saying something like, "I don't know if you already thought about this. . . ." But she may be ignored no matter how she speaks.

5   I also discovered that if a man and a woman talk the same amount at a meeting, people will think the woman talked too much. All of this indicates that, for the most part, conversations in the workplace are still conducted according to boys' rules.

After You Read

Use the paraphrasing skills you learned in the Language Learning Strategy to paraphrase the reading orally with a partner.

Discussion Questions

1. What is the communication style of women in the workplace? How does this affect their work?

2. In what way is the workplace still conducted by the "boys' rules"?

3. Can you think of any other ways that the communication style of women could cause problems for them at work?

4. Have you ever experienced difficulty with communication between men and women at work?

Getting Ready to Listen

In each of the following conversations on the tape, there is a breakdown in communication. These breakdowns are similar to those you heard in the chapter on communication between cultures; however, the source of the breakdown in this chapter is found in gender stereotypes. As you listen, first try to identify the behavior that is related to gender stereotypes. Use your note-taking skills to focus your listening. Refer to your list of stereotypes to help you. Next, try to think of ways the speakers could have asked for clarification and expressed empathy to avoid the misunderstanding. Then, answer the questions that refer to each dialogue.

◆ **Listen**

Listening 1: Gender Stereotypes

Dialogue 1: "The New Haircut"

1. What are these people in conflict about?

   _____

2. What does the man in the situation want?

   _____

3. What does the woman in the situation want?

   _____

4. What is one place in the conversation that someone asks for clarification? What is said? Is clarification received?

   _____

5. What is one place in the conversation that someone could have expressed empathy? What could he or she have said?

   _____

Dialogue 2: "The Cocktail Bar Job Discussion"

1. What are these people in conflict about?

   _____

2. What does the man in the situation want?

   _____

3. What does the woman in the situation want?

   _____

4. What is one place in the conversation that someone could have asked for clarification? What could he or she have said?

   _____

5. What is one place in the conversation that someone could have expressed empathy? What could he or she have said?

   _____

Dialogue 3: "I Can Handle It Myself!"

1. What are these people in conflict about?

   _____

2. What does the man in the situation want?

   _____

3. What does the woman in the situation want?

   _____

4. What is one place in the conversation that someone could have asked for clarification? What could he or she have said?

   _____

5. What is one place in the conversation that someone could have expressed empathy? What could he or she have said?

   _____

Dialogue 4: "Do You Always Have to Cry?"

1. What are these people in conflict about?

   _____

2. What does the man in the situation want?

   _____

3. What does the woman in the situation want?

   _____

4. What is one place in the conversation that someone could have asked for clarification? What could he or she have said?

   _____

5. What is one place in the conversation that someone could have expressed empathy? What could he or she have said?

   _____

After You Listen

Write About It.

You have been discussing the communication problems that men and women experience based on gender stereotyping and communication styles. Based on this discussion, how will you approach your relationships differently? What kinds of changes will you make in the way you communicate with members of the opposite sex? Write about this on the lines below.

_____

_____

_____

_____

_____

REAL PEOPLE/REAL VOICES

 Getting Ready to Listen

You are going to hear a tape with real people discussing their communication problems with members of the opposite sex. Before you listen, think about your own experiences. Try to remember one situation where you had the kinds of communication problems you've been discussing in this chapter. Take turns with your partner describing each of your situations. After your partner describes his/her situation, clarify what the problem was. Then, express empathy with your partner. Finally, suggest how your partner could have solved the problem.

My Partner

Problem: _____

_____

Solution: _____

_____

 Listen

Listening 2: Marty's, Sharon's, and Chris's Experiences

You are going to hear a tape with real people discussing their communication problems with members of the opposite sex. First, Marty talks about her husband's lack of interest in her clothes. Then, Sharon explains a problem that she experiences with her boyfriend, who doesn't like to talk much. Finally, Chris discusses a problem he had with a woman he was dating. As you listen, take notes. For each speaker, paraphrase the problem.

Marty's Problem _____

_____

Sharon's Problem _____

_____

Chris's Problem _____

_____

◆After You Listen

With a small group, share your paraphrase of each problem on the tape. As you share each paraphrase, discuss the reason for the problem. Then discuss with your group members how each person could solve the problem. Come to an agreement on the best solution.

Solution for Marty _____

_____

Solution for Sharon _____

_____

Solution for Chris _____

_____

PUTTING IT ALL TOGETHER
. . . .

Work with your classmates to complete the following tasks. Write your answers on the lines provided. This activity will help to list and measure the things you learned in this chapter.

1. In each of the following dialogues, ask for clarification, give clarification, and express empathy.

   a. Woman: "You never listen to me."

   Man (ask for clarification): _____

   Woman (give clarification): _____

   Man (express empathy): _____

   b. Man: "We don't spend enough time together."

   Woman (ask for clarification): _____

   Man (give clarification): _____

   Woman (express empathy): _____

2. List two ways you can improve communication with members of the opposite sex:

   a. _____

   b. _____

3. List two ways in which you participated more actively during this class session:

   a. _____

   b. _____

4. Write one question that you had about the topic before this class session. What is the answer to the question?

   _____

Test-Taking Tip

Stay calm. You can't answer questions correctly if you are frantic. If you feel nervous, relax by taking a few deep breaths. Maintain your confidence; attitude can affect your performance.

CHECK YOUR PROGRESS

On a scale of 1 to 5, rate how well you have mastered the goals set at the beginning of the chapter:

1 2 3 4 5   plan in advance in order to get the most out of each class session.

1 2 3 4 5   take notes as you observe and listen to a conversation.

1 2 3 4 5   ask for clarification.

1 2 3 4 5   give clarification of your point of view.

1 2 3 4 5   paraphrase what someone communicates to you.

1 2 3 4 5   communicate more effectively with members of the opposite sex.

1 2 3 4 5   express empathy for another person's feelings.

If you've given yourself a 3 or lower on any of these goals:

- visit the *Tapestry* web site for additional practice.
- ask your instructor for extra help.
- review the sections of the chapter that you found difficult.
- work with a partner or study group to further your progress.

The Berlin Wall was built after World War II to separate East Berlin from West Berlin. Now the wall has been taken down, and Berlin is one city. Can you think of any other boundaries like this that still exist in the world? What are the reasons for such boundaries? What are the disadvantages of this kind of boundary?

4

CROSSING THE LINE

Communication is very often a way to exchange information or share thoughts and feelings that bring you closer to others. In addition, one of the most basic reasons for communicating is to get things that you need. You attempt to meet these needs in a couple of different ways. You may make a simple request or, if the need is very strong, make demands of other people. In this chapter, you will examine how people and governments negotiate. You will use the skills you learned in the previous chapter about resolving conflict between individuals. You will apply those skills to situations involving conflict between countries and governments. In Chapter Three we discussed how we must learn certain communication skills to make our personal relationships work well. These skills include negotiation, compromise, and understanding the point of view of another person. Do you think these same skills are important when a problem occurs between two governments or two countries? How do you think the world might be different if people learned to negotiate in better ways? Discuss these questions with a partner.

Setting Goals

In this chapter you will learn how to:

- make direct requests.
- state implicit demands.
- state a refusal.
- offer a polite excuse.
- identify a speaker's intent.
- use key words to improve your note taking.
- cooperate with classmates during group work.

◆Getting Started

Think about your awareness of other countries by answering the following questions. There are no right or wrong answers. The purpose of this activity is to examine your beliefs, attitudes, and feelings. After you have completed the statements by yourself, discuss your answers with a partner.

What Do I Know About the Topic?

1. How much do you think you know about other countries?

   a lot   enough   a little

2. How much do you think you *need* to know about other countries?

   a lot   enough   a little

3. Why do you need to know about other countries?

4. What do you need to know about other countries? Why?

5. What kinds of problems result from not knowing enough about other countries?

What Do I Know About the Language?

1. If you wanted to **request** that someone move his or her car from your parking space, what would you say?

   _____

   _____

   _____

   _____

   _____

   _____

2. If you wanted to **demand** that someone move his or her car from your parking space, what would you say?

   _____

   _____

   _____

   _____

   _____

   _____

3. How is the request you wrote different from the demand? Can the same words be used for both? How will the listener know whether it's a request or a demand?

_____

_____

4. In your native language, is there a difference between making a request and stating a demand? What is this difference?

_____

_____

PART 1: Boundary? What's a Boundary?

WARMING UP: OUR WORLD—YESTERDAY, TODAY . . . AND TOMORROW

Sometimes, people believe that the world will always be as it is today. However, the briefest look at history shows that the boundaries you may consider to be permanent are in fact always changing because of the changing needs of people. Form a group and answer the following questions about the maps on the following pages.

1. To help your group learn, point out your native country on the current map. Have the boundaries of your country changed?

2. What are the changes in the boundaries of your country? Why did these changes occur?

3. What other differences do you notice on these maps? With your group, find five differences.

4. Why did these changes occur? What was happening in the world at this time?

5. With your group, think of at least six reasons why boundary changes occur (for example, an invasion).

6. Now that you have looked at the global concept of boundaries, what is meant by the concept of personal boundaries? Does any link exist between these two concepts? What is it?

The world in 1914

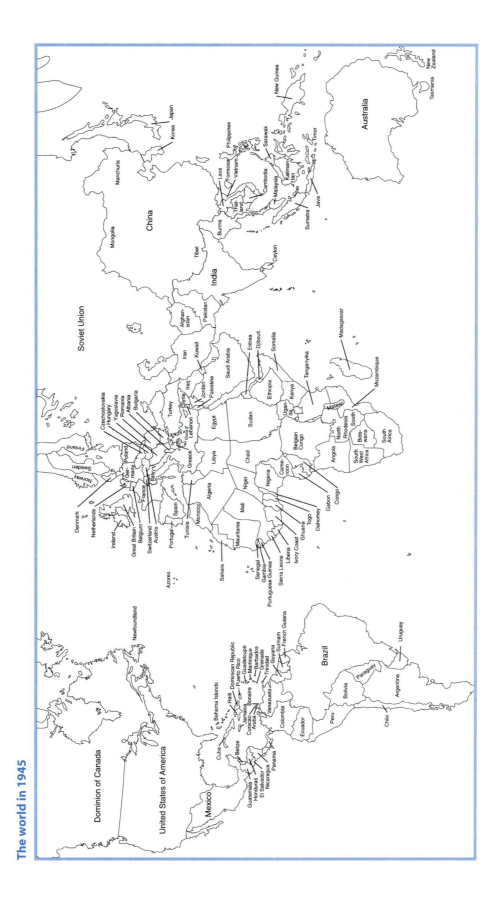

The world in 1945

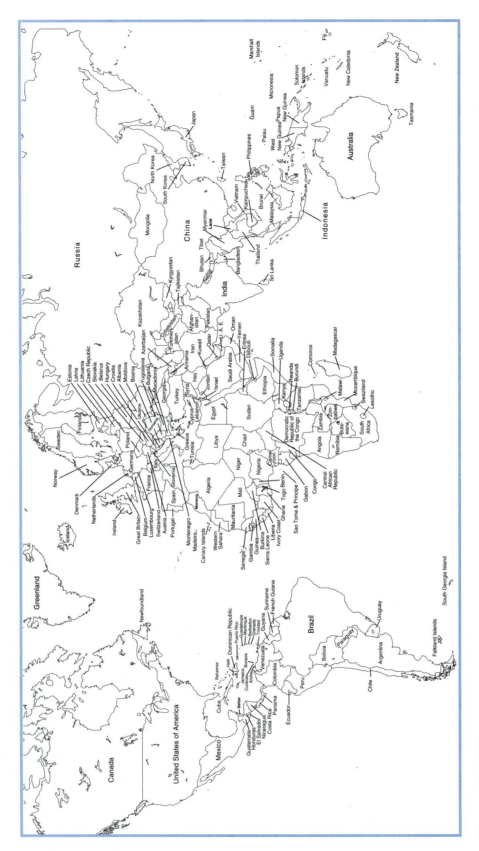

The world in 1999

◆ Getting Ready to Read

Discussion

You are going to read a short article about boundaries. The article discusses how boundaries that have always kept us separate are changing and disappearing. How do you think our lives will change in the future if the boundaries that keep us separate continue to disappear? Discuss with a partner how life will change if the following boundaries disappear:

geographical boundaries (people move freely from one geographical location to another.)

class boundaries (people are not separated by social or economic class.)

religious boundaries (people can belong to any religion regardless of their nationality or location.)

spatial boundaries (people can communicate with anyone, anywhere in the world, whenever they want.)

◆ Read

One World, Many Universes

1   This is, in many ways, a world without boundaries . . . Being a citizen of a particular nation means about as much as being a resident of a particular county or province. The freedom of people to move increases gradually with the relaxation of immigration laws. Most countries have fairly simple requirements for obtaining citizenship and voting rights. Boundaries of class and caste that once shaped societies continue to fade. Marxism has withered away too, along with other rigid ideologies that once served as props of personal identity. All of the major organized religions—including Christianity, Judaism, Buddhism, Hinduism, and Islam—are alive and well, but no longer clearly and exclusively identified with specific cultures and geographic regions. People everywhere feel free to convert to other religions, and many people identify with more than one religion. Cyberspace has become a rich and realistic realm of experience. Its activities include the No-Self Network, which is concerned with liberation from the self. The network's members regard this liberation as an ordinary human achievement—roughly comparable to learning to play the piano—and not as a superhuman or divine feat. One World, Many Universes is, for me, the most persuasive mix of idealism and realism. This particular future is likely to be the most fast-changing one, rapidly evolving beyond what I have described.

 **After You Read**

Oral Paraphrase

Below are some of the words and phrases from the reading. Next to the words and phrases are synonyms which help you to understand the meaning. Find each word or phrase in the reading and underline it. Then read through the article again orally with a partner. Take turns with your partner and paraphrase each sentence. Use the synonyms for the underlined words and phrases as you paraphrase. Use the other paraphrasing skills you practiced in Chapter Three.

class and caste: social position or group
withered away: slowly disappeared
rigid ideologies: strict belief systems
props: support
personal identity: who you are
convert: change from one religion to another
realm of experience: environment or place to experience something
liberation from the self: feeling free
superhuman or divine feat: beyond an ordinary human accomplishment
rapidly evolving: quickly changing
persuasive mix of idealism and realism: believable combination of fantasy and reality

Where Do Your Personal Boundaries Lie?

Now you will have an opportunity to see the similarity between the global and personal concepts of boundaries. Look at the following situations. See how comfortable you would feel in each of these situations involving negotiations and boundaries.

Following are several situations and, after each, five emotions that you might feel in those situations. Individually, read each one and circle any emotion you think you would feel if this truly happened to you. After you finish, discuss your answers with your group.

Situation 1: It's the day of the big essay exam. You have studied hard, so you are well prepared. A few minutes before the test begins, your classmate informs you that she has forgotten her dictionary. This classmate asks if it would be possible to share your dictionary during the exam. As the exam progresses, your classmate repeatedly borrows your dictionary.

generous   accommodating   nervous   threatened   angry

other _____ (explain)

Situation 2: You are in a coffee shop doing some homework. Your papers are spread out on the table. A stranger comes up and sits down without asking. To accommodate the stranger, you must give up some of your workspace.

generous   accommodating   nervous   threatened   angry

other _____ (explain)

Situation 3: One day you drive into your driveway and notice that your neighbor has put up a fence to divide his property from yours. In doing so, he has built the fence so far in that you have lost some property. You weren't really using that land, but it is legally yours.

generous   accommodating   nervous   threatened   angry

other _____ (explain)

Situation 4: You work in a company where there is limited office space, and all offices are assigned by management. A co-worker has moved into your office without anyone's permission. Because of the limited space in your office, you find it difficult to maneuver.

generous   accommodating   nervous   threatened   angry

other _____ (explain)

Situation 5: You are renting an upstairs apartment. Your downstairs neighbor frequently plays very loud music, which disturbs you.

generous   accommodating   nervous   threatened   angry

other _____ (explain)

Situation 6: You and a roommate have recently moved into an apartment. Your roommate frequently uses your things without asking.

generous   accommodating   nervous   threatened   angry

other _____ (explain)

In these situations you have imagined how you might feel when another person accidentally (or perhaps knowingly) violates your personal boundaries. In English we call this *stepping on someone's toes*. Do you have a similar expression in your native language? Share it with your group.

What Would You Say?

Choose two of the previous situations that caused you to feel threat-ened or angry. What would you say in each of these situations? What do you think would happen after you said that? With your group, dis-cuss some of your ideas. In the grid below, write down two or three of your favorite choices. An example is provided for you in the first box.

Situation	What Would You Say?	Expected Result
Situation 2: The Coffee Shop	"Would you mind moving? I need this space so that I can work."	The stranger would apologize and move.

The example in the chart uses a request form: "Would you mind moving?" How-ever, the speaker is actually making a de-mand. Do people also phrase demands as requests in your native culture? Why would someone do this? People from the United States consider it extremely rude to give someone a direct order to do something. Therefore, a request is often made when, in fact, the speaker is imply-ing a demand. In the next part of the chapter, you will focus on this language.

Write About It.

Think about a time when you had a conflict with someone. What was the conflict? How did it feel to have that conflict? How did you resolve the conflict? Did you have a mediator? Do you think you could have resolved the conflict more successfully if you had known about some techniques of conflict resolution? Write about this on the lines below.

_____

_____

_____

_____

_____

_____

_____

_____

PART 2: Stepping on Toes (Ouch!)

. . . .

LANGUAGE YOU CAN USE: STATING A REQUEST, REFUSING A DEMAND, AND OFFERING AN EXCUSE

. . . .

 Physically, when someone steps on your toes, you probably don't hesitate to indicate that you are uncomfortable. You may say something as simple as "Ouch!" to alert that person to your discomfort or something more subtle and complex, like "Pardon me, but you've accidentally stepped on my foot." However, it's much more difficult to express your feelings when someone steps on your toes emotionally or politically. Below are some expressions that can be used to state a specific demand or to refuse when someone else has made a demand on you.

STATING A REQUEST/IMPLYING A DEMAND

Situation	Stating a Request	Implicit Demand
Your area is in a drought. You need water now. The neighboring land has surplus water.	**Would you mind giving us some water?** **It would help us** if you gave us some water.	**Give** us your extra water. (We need it more than you do.)
You were absent from class for one week. Your classmate takes very good notes.	**I could sure use** your notes. **I'd really appreciate it if** you lent me your notes.	You **must** lend me your notes.

REFUSING A DEMAND

Situation	Refusing a Demand
Your area has surplus water.	**I'm sorry, but** you can't have it.
Your classmate often misses class and expects to get help from others by using their notes.	**I'm sorry, but I can't** lend you my notes.

OFFERING AN EXCUSE

Situation	Offering An Excuse
Your neighbors want your surplus water. However, your population has expanded rapidly. You must develop new agricultural land. You plan to use your surplus water in the near future.	**We'd really like to help you out, but** we're going to need that water.
Your friend wants to borrow your notes. You do not want to lend them to her, but you are not comfortable saying that.	**I sure wish I could, but** I need to study them. **Not this time because** I need them. **Maybe next time.**

People in the United States often feel a little guilty if they have to say no to a request. It is therefore quite common for them to offer an excuse to explain why they have said no. Immediately after voicing their refusal, they will offer their excuse. Do you do the same thing?

USING NEW LANGUAGE

With a partner, read each of the following situations. Take turns making requests of each other. If you definitely expect your partner to honor your request, be aware of how you use your voice to convey this message. Practice refusing as well. Try to offer excuses when you feel they are necessary.

1. You leave your seat in a crowded movie theater because you need a drink of water. Your jacket remains draped over the seat to show that someone is sitting there. When you return, you find that someone has taken your place. You want to ask this person to vacate your seat.

2. While reading a magazine article in class, you find many words that you do not understand. Unfortunately, you have forgotten your dictionary. The student next to you has a dictionary that you would like to use to complete the reading.

3. While you are standing in line for the bus, someone steps in front of you.

4. You share a crowded office with several other people. You must all share one computer. Your office mate is working on the computer, but you need to use it soon to prepare an assignment.

5. You are in the shower. Your roommate asks you to hurry so that she can get into the bathroom to shower as well. You need a few more minutes to finish up.

LISTEN FOR INTENT

 Getting Ready to Listen

Read and discuss the "Language Learning Strategy" below. This strategy will prepare you to understand the intent of a speaker when you hear a conversation.

LANGUAGE LEARNING STRATEGY

Identify a speaker's intent, and you will understand what is being asked of you. In English, sometimes we use words that mean one thing, but the message we truly want to communicate may be something different. It is important that you learn to identify a speaker's intent. Then you will understand what is being asked of you. Listen to the volume of the speaker. Demands are usually louder than requests. Listen to the tone of the speaker. Demands sound stronger and less polite than requests. Identify what the intent of the speaker is. If the speaker doesn't expect the listener to refuse but expects the listener to do what is being asked, it is a *demand*. If the speaker isn't sure whether the listener will do what is being asked, it is a *request*.

Apply the Strategy

As you do the listening activity below, use what you learned in this "Language Learning Strategy" to identify the speaker's intent. Notice the volume that is used by the speaker who is making a request. Also, listen to the tone of the speaker and determine whether the tone is strong and aggressive or soft and polite. Then identify what the intent of the speaker is.

 Listen

Listening 1: Listen for Intent

Listen to each of the short conversations. For each conversation, choose the answer that best identifies the speaker's intent.

Conversation 1

a. **Volume**   b. **Tone**

_____ loud   _____ strong/not polite

_____ normal   _____ soft/polite

c. **Intent**

_____ Adolfo is demanding that Tri share his book. He doesn't expect him to refuse.

_____ Adolfo is requesting that Tri share his book. He is not sure whether he will agree to that.

Conversation 2

a. **Volume**   b. **Tone**

_____ loud   _____ strong/not polite

_____ normal   _____ soft/polite

c. **Intent**

_____ Sandra is demanding that Richard let her know before taking the computer out of the office, and she doesn't expect him to refuse.

_____ Sandra is requesting that Richard let her know before taking the computer out of the office, but she is not sure whether he will agree.

Conversation 3

a. **Volume**   b. **Tone**

_____ loud   _____ strong/not polite

_____ normal   _____ soft/polite

c. **Intent**

_____ Mr. Sarkis is demanding that Ms. Arawan give him more time. He doesn't expect her to refuse.

_____ Mr. Sarkis is requesting that Ms. Arawan give him more time. He is not sure whether she will agree to that.

Conversation 4

a. **Volume**   b. **Tone**

_____ loud   _____ strong/not polite

_____ normal   _____ soft/polite

c. **Intent**

_____ Lucia is demanding that Christina do the revisions. She doesn't expect her to refuse.

_____ Lucia is requesting that Christina do the revisions. She is not sure whether Christina will be able to do them.

Conversation 5

a. **Volume**

_____ loud

_____ normal

b. **Tone**

_____ strong/not polite

_____ soft/polite

c. **Intent**

_____ Bill is demanding that Sonja give the group the data by Friday. He doesn't expect her to refuse.

_____ Bill is requesting that Sonja give the group the data by Friday. He is not sure whether she will agree to that.

◆ After You Listen

> **Pick battles big enough to matter, small enough to win.**
>
> **—JONATHAN KOZOL**

After you listen to the conversations, compare your answers with a partner. Then, after you agree on the speaker's intent, you will hear the conversations one more time. Decide with your partner how the listener should respond to the request in each conversation. Write your response on the lines below.

Conversation 1

Adolfo: Excuse me, Tri. Did you bring your book today?
Tri: Yes, I did. Why?
Adolfo: I forgot my book today and we're going to review for the quiz. Would you mind sharing your book with me while we do the review?

Tri: _____

Conversation 2

Richard: Hi, Sandra.
Sandra: Hi, Richard.
Richard: How are you doing?
Sandra: I'm OK, but you know I have to say, I'm a little irritated. You took the computer out of the office yesterday for your seminar, and I was stuck here with no computer. I'd really appreciate it if you'd let me know in the future if you want to take the computer out of the office.

Richard: _____

_____

Conversation 3

Ms. Arawan: Well, Mr. Sarkis, that's what we can offer you. I think you'll agree that it is a very generous offer. So perhaps we can sign the agreement now?

Mr. Sarkis: It would help us if you gave us more time to speak with our council members about these negotiations before we reach a final decision.

Ms. Arawan: _____

_____

_____

Conversation 4

Lucia: This proposal is ready to be signed. I'm glad we finished it before the end of the week.

Christina: Me too! That was a lot of work, but I think we did a good job.

Lucia: Yes, I think so too. Listen, would you mind doing the final revisions while I go meet with the sales team?

Christina: _____

_____

_____

Conversation 5

Bill: Well, the group is almost finished with this project, but we're still waiting for the data that you were supposed to gather.

Sonja: Yes, I know, but I've had three tests this week, and I'm feeling really overloaded right now.

Bill: I understand, but as you know this project is due very soon. We could sure use those statistics by Friday so that we don't miss the deadline.

Sonja: _____

_____

_____

CONFLICT RESOLUTION

◆ **Getting Ready to Listen**   Read and discuss the "Language Learning Strategy" on the next page. This strategy will prepare you to take better notes when you listen to a conversation or other listening passage.

LANGUAGE LEARNING STRATEGY

U se key words to improve your note taking. When you take notes, you are creating an effective study guide for yourself. Write down key words in the margin when you hear them. Key words are the words that express the main ideas or important facts of the lecture. If you write the key words in the margin, then when you study, you will remember the most important ideas you heard in the lecture. When you are studying for a test or getting ready for a class discussion, use the key words to help you prepare.

Apply the Strategy

As you do the listening activity below, use what you learned in this "Language Learning Strategy" to take better notes.

conflict

resolution

communication

Listen

Listening 2: Conflict Resolution

Listen to the taped interview about conflict resolution. During the interview, several steps for resolving conflict will be discussed. As you listen, take notes below about each of the steps described. Some comments have been included after the title of each step to help you focus your listening. Write key words and main ideas in the left margin to improve your note taking.

Step One: Setting up a positive environment (this step has two parts)

Key Words	Notes
_____	_____
_____	_____
_____	_____

_____   _____

_____   _____

Step Two: Identifying the bottom line (the mediator helps people identify two different things)

Key Words   **Notes**

_____   _____

_____   _____

_____   _____

_____   _____

_____   _____

Step Three: Brainstorming (there are two steps in the process of brainstorming)

Key Words   **Notes**

_____   _____

_____   _____

_____   _____

_____   _____

_____   _____

Step Four: Writing a shared commitment (the clients need to complete a specific task in this step)

Key Words   **Notes**

_____   _____

_____   _____

_____   _____

_____   _____

_____   _____

 **After You Listen**

Practice the mediation counseling skills you've learned to resolve conflicts. Form groups of three. Choose one person to be the mediator and two to be clients. Choose one of the following situations to resolve. The mediator will help the clients solve the conflict by using the steps described in the lecture. You may use your notes to help you.

Situation 1: The Roommate Dilemma

Two roommates have a conflict about house-work. One of them doesn't clean up after herself. The other is always cleaning up for both.

Situation 2: The Loud Officemate

Two colleagues have a problem sharing their office. One of them is extremely loud and spends a lot of time chatting and telling jokes when the other is trying to work. The other officemate is frequently distracted by the uncomfortable noise level.

REAL PEOPLE/REAL VOICES

◆ **Getting Ready to Listen**

You are going to hear two students talking about boundaries. They are going to answer this question: "Would you like to live in a world with no boundaries?" Discuss the following questions with your classmates before you listen to the tape:

1. Has your native country ever been divided into parts?

2. How do you imagine it feels to live in a country that has been divided—e.g., Korea?

3. What are the disadvantages of boundaries that separate the same country?

4. What do you think it would be like to live in a world without boundaries? Do you think this is possible? Why or why not?

◆ **Listen**

Listening 3: Doo-Won's and Katica's Experiences

As you listen to the tape, write down three demands that each student makes.

Speaker 1: Doo-Won

1. _____

2. _____

3. _____

Speaker 2: Katica

1. _____

2. _____

3. _____

After You Listen

Discussion: Compare the comments of Doo-Won and Katica with the answers you gave before you heard the tape. Did you share the feelings they had about living in a world without boundaries?

The Sound of It: Distinguishing Syllables

Each of the words below is taken from "Real People/Real Voices." Each of the words has three syllables. First, mark where the syllables are divided. Then listen to the tape again. Because of reduction, some of the words are pronounced with two syllables. As you listen, mark if the word is pronounced with two or three syllables.

1. Divide syllables

   a. boundaries

   b. suffering

   c. dangerous

   d. torturing

   e. agreement

   f. creating

2. Listen for the reductions

   a. _____ 2   _____ 3

   b. _____ 2   _____ 3

   c. _____ 2   _____ 3

   d. _____ 2   _____ 3

   e. _____ 2   _____ 3

   f. _____ 2   _____ 3

PAIRED ACTIVITY: BOUNDARY ISSUES 1

You are a member of a negotiating team for your country. In each of the following situations, you are involved in a dispute over resources with a representative from another country. There are demands that

> Talking of patriotism, what humbug it is; it is a word which always commemorates a robbery. There isn't a foot of land in the world which doesn't represent the ousting and re-ousting of a long line of successive owners.
>
> —MARK TWAIN

each of the representatives can make in each situation. Take turns with your partner making and refusing the demands.

Situation 1: Building in the Buffer Zone

An area of your country has traditionally served as a buffer zone between yours and a neighboring country, with which you have a hostile relationship. A recent wave of immigrants has made it necessary for you to build a great deal of new housing. You don't have much space, and your government has decided to build in the buffer zone even though this may seem threatening to your neighbor.

Situation 2: The Oil Crisis

You are an oil-poor country bordering a country rich in oil. You have recently discovered oil on your land near the border. You wish to drill for this oil. You have no idea how large the oil reservoir is, but it may extend into the land of the neighboring country.

Situation 3: Hunger Strikes

Your country is in a state of famine. You are receiving aid from an international relief organization. People from the neighboring country are crossing your border and stealing this food from the warehouses. This country is capable of producing enough food to feed its own population. However, this country is involved in a civil war. Troops frequently burn down crops to punish villagers whom they suspect of supporting the other side.

Situation 4: Don't Rain on My Parade

You represent a heavily industrialized nation that sells much of what you manufacture to a neighboring country at a very low price because they buy in large quantity. Unfortunately, the pollution from your factories is contributing to the acid-rain problem. This acid rain falls heavily on the neighboring country. This country is very concerned and has asked you to take expensive steps toward making your factories environmentally safe.

Situation 5: Run River Run

A river flows across your border with a neighboring country, which is quite poor and has very low quality municipal services. This country does not have adequate sewage treatment plants, so much of the raw sewage is piped directly into the river and flows into your country.

TUNING IN: "The Ellis Island Decision"

© CNN

Discuss the following questions with your classmates before you watch the video.

1. Do you know where Ellis Island is?

2. What is Ellis Island famous for?

3. What do you think should happen if a historical landmark is shared geographically by two cities?

You will watch a video about a decision that was made by the U.S. Supreme Court concerning Ellis Island. As you watch the video the first time, listen to find out what decision was made.

The Supreme Court's decision was _____

_____

_____

_____

As you listen a second time, read the statements below. Write **NY** if the statement is true about New York and **NJ** if the statement is true about New Jersey.

_____ It claimed Ellis Island on historic precedent.

_____ It claimed Ellis Island based on an 1834 treaty.

_____ It will own the original 3-acre section including the main building.

_____ It will own most of the 27-acre island—the part built on landfill.

As you listen a third time, write **T** if the statement is true and **F** if the statement is false.

_____ Ellis Island was the destination for 13 million immigrants.

_____ Ellis Island was the destination for many immigrants between 1892 and 1954.

_____ Ellis Island was originally called Ellis Island, New York.

_____ Ellis Island is visited by 1,000 people every year.

_____ New York has collected $300,000 in sales tax in the past.

_____ Many people think the Supreme Court decision was silly.

Discussion

What do you think about the decision that was made about Ellis Island? Do you think that it is right for a political boundary to divide a historical landmark in this way?

ACADEMIC POWER STRATEGY

Cooperate with classmates during group work. When you are asked to work with a group of classmates, you will accomplish the task more successfully if you cooperate. Follow these steps to cooperate:

1. Allow a group leader to manage the group.

2. Listen to the opinions of others.

3. Participate in the discussion, and state *your* opinions.

4. Work together to solve problems.

Apply the Strategy

As you work on the group activity below, follow the steps that you learned in the "Academic Power Strategy" to cooperate better with your classmates during group work.

GROUP ACTIVITY: BOUNDARY ISSUES 2

April 25, 1945 – Britain, China, the Soviet Union, and the United States call a conference in San Francisco at which the United Nations is officially established.

You are attending a conference for international peace. Your teacher will assign you to be a representative of a specific country.* You will sit in a group with the other representatives of your country. Read the description, and with your group members fill in the grid on the next page to indicate what you need from the other countries. (Do not read the descriptions of the other countries.) After you complete the grid, you will send an ambassador from your country to one of the other countries to negotiate for what you need. The ambassador should make a deal and return back to the group to report the progress.

*See pages 224–226 for descriptions.

My Country:	
Country 1:	Need:
Country 2:	Need:
Country 3:	Need:
Country 4:	Need:

PUTTING IT ALL TOGETHER

1. List two things that you learned in this chapter about other countries:

   _____

   _____

   _____

2. Make an implicit demand for each situation below.

   a. You want your classmate to stop talking because you can't hear the teacher speaking.

   _____

   b. You want your co-worker to come back from lunch break on time so that you can take your break.

   _____

3. Refuse each of the demands in #2 and give an excuse.

   a. _____

   b _____

4. Write two of the four steps you learned for conflict resolution.

   a. _____

   b _____

Test-Taking Tip

Pay attention to all the information available to you at the start of the test. Pay especially close attention to verbal instructions. Then, read the directions on the test slowly and carefully. If there is anything you are confused about in the instructions, ask your teacher for clarification.

CHECK YOUR PROGRESS

On a scale of 1 to 5, rate how well you have mastered the goals set at the beginning of the chapter:

1 2 3 4 5   make direct requests.

1 2 3 4 5   state implicit demands.

1 2 3 4 5   state a refusal.

1 2 3 4 5   offer a polite excuse.

1 2 3 4 5   identify a speaker's intent.

1 2 3 4 5   use key words to improve your note taking.

1 2 3 4 5   cooperate with classmates during group work.

If you've given yourself a 3 or lower on any of these goals:

- visit the *Tapestry* web site for additional practice.
- ask your instructor for extra help.
- review the sections of the chapter that you found difficult.
- work with a partner or study group to further your progress.

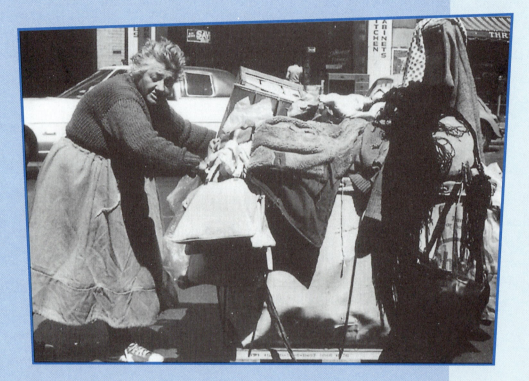

Even in the best of economic times, there will always be some people who do not have everything that they need to survive comfortably.

- Are there a lot of homeless people in your area?
- How do you feel when you see a homeless person?
- What are some things that you think individuals and governments can do to help homeless people?

MY SLICE OF THE PIE

In Chapter Four, you discussed how difficult it can be to negotiate when people and/or nations are trying to make sure that their needs are met. Sometimes, it is clearly impossible to satisfy everyone. This can cause you to question yourselves, your social institutions, perhaps even your governments. In Chapter Five, you will discuss what can happen to societies and individuals in a world where we all compete daily for resources. The language skills that people use to talk about important needs and ask for advice in the world of economic issues are similar to the language skills that students use to get help and advice in order to do good work in their classrooms and schools. It's the language to use for getting what you need.

Setting Goals

In this chapter you will learn how to:

◈ express needs so you can ask for what is important to you.

◈ improve your ability to remember.

◈ offer advice in order to help others get what they need.

◈ identify the most important words in a sentence by listening for emphasis.

◈ listen for the language of advice and suggestion so you know when others are trying to help you.

◈ practice or repeat new language to make the language more familiar and comfortable.

◆Getting Started

77% of persons below the poverty level live in metropolitan areas.

—U.S. CENSUS BUREAU

Before you begin the activities in this chapter, take a few minutes to think about what you want and/or need to know about this topic.

What Do I Know About the Topic?

1. Are you often aware of those who are suffering economically?

2. Do you feel it is important for you to have a clear understanding of why these problems occur in your native culture and in other cultures?

3. Why is it necessary to be able to talk about problems in our world or at school?

4. Why is it necessary to be able to ask for what you need at school?

What Do I Know About the Language?

1. Is it important to be able to talk about problems in English? Why?

2. Is it important to be able to use English to give good advice to people about problems? Why?

3. What is the best way to give advice to other people?

4. Do you know when someone is offering a suggestion or giving you advice in English?

VALUES CLARIFICATION

Look at each statement below. Circle your response to the statement. Think about why you chose each response. Having a clear idea of your own attitudes makes it easier to plan for and measure your progress.

1. It is the responsibility of a government to provide for all the basic needs of its citizens.

strongly agree   agree   agree somewhat   disagree   strongly disagree

2. Each individual is basically responsible for himself. It is not good to rely on others for support.

strongly agree   agree   agree somewhat   disagree   strongly disagree

3. By helping others we help ourselves.

strongly agree   agree   agree somewhat   disagree   strongly disagree

4. Helping other people makes them weak and dependent.

strongly agree   agree   agree somewhat   disagree   strongly disagree

5. If a society takes care of all its members, the society becomes strong and successful.

strongly agree   agree   agree somewhat   disagree   strongly disagree

6. It is impossible and unnatural to provide for everyone.

strongly agree   agree   agree somewhat   disagree   strongly disagree

7. It is the responsibility of a good teacher to provide for all the needs of his or her students.

strongly agree   agree   agree somewhat   disagree   strongly disagree

8. It is possible for all students to succeed in school.

strongly agree   agree   agree somewhat   disagree   strongly disagree

9. It is impossible for a teacher to know what every student needs.

strongly agree   agree   agree somewhat   disagree   strongly disagree

10. All students need the same things to succeed in school.

strongly agree   agree   agree somewhat   disagree   strongly disagree

PART 1: Seeking Shelter from the Storm— Helping People in Need

Discussion

After completing the values-clarification activity above, work with a partner. Begin by reading the questions below and using them to discuss the statements in the values-clarification exercise.

1. What does each statement mean? Do you and your partner agree on the meaning?

2. Why did you choose your responses?

3. Do you think some of these statements are in conflict? Which ones? Why?

REAL PEOPLE/REAL VOICES

Getting Ready to Listen   **Vocabulary Building**

The sentences below use vocabulary and idioms from the conversation you will hear. Look at these in context, and circle the answer that you think gives the best definition.

1. The information people need isn't **at their fingertips.**

    a) difficult to get

    b) easily available

    c) on a computer

2. One mistake people make is **to live paycheck to paycheck.**

    a) just paying bills when money comes in, never able to save

    b) using cash only

    c) using credit cards

3. People born between 1945 and 1964 are part of the **baby boomer** generation. They are a big part of the population now.

    a) a period of time with high birth rates

    b) middle-aged

    c) middle class

4. To save money you should always **pay yourself first.**

    a) spend on the things you want before you save

    b) spend as little as possible

    c) pay your savings account like you pay a bill

5. Some things, like retirement, you can plan for. Other things, like getting sick, **rise up unexpectedly.**

    a) happen at a certain time

    b) arrive on time

    c) occur without plan

Listen   **Listening 1: Grace's Experience**

Grace is the president of an all-women's investment group. She has a master's in business administration and worked in the area of investment for ten years. Listen to the interview. Grace talks about planning for emergencies. Fill in the missing words.

Q: Do you think _____ today do a good job of planning for _____ emergencies?

A: Well, I think _____ people want to have a secure _____. Um, however, the information they need, um, to _____ financial security isn't at their _____. Um, okay, for example, well, they need to establish their goals, for instance, how much _____ do you need to live, what would be a _____ amount that you need to live? They have to take things like whether they want to pay for their _____ to go to college, which college they're going to go to, um, and many people in the _____ boomer group are faced with having to care for a _____, which is an added expense and has to be, um, considered in any future financial _____.

Q: Then how much money do you _____ people need to save for themselves?

A: Well, the thing is, you should have 3–6 _____ of monthly salary saved, so whatever your monthly _____ is you should have enough to pay your expenses for 3–6 months without any income.

Q: And then in _____ to that, most of us need to plan for college, _____, taking care of parents, etc?

A: Uh-huh. And the kinds of things that _____ (2 words) unexpectedly, for example, like the _____ heater blowing up or the car not starting in the morning.

Q: So, what's the _____ mistake people make?

A: Well, they tend to live from _____ to paycheck. And when something unexpectedly _____, if they don't have someone to help, they just go deeper and deeper into _____, you fall farther and farther behind in your payments. Or, it gets so bad that you _____ everything, like what has happened to many people who are forced into homelessness and are there because their debts became overwhelming.

Q: So, if you could give people one piece of _____ to make their financial future more secure, what would you suggest?

A: Younger people often _____ every last cent that they earn. They live from paycheck to paycheck. After they pay

> I finally know what distinguishes man from the other beasts: financial worries.
>
> —JULES RENARD

their bills, they _____ that there's nothing left over to save. The best advice I can give is to say "Pay yourself first." When you get your paycheck, save some _____ of it, even $10 a week. That's giving up a movie, and one stop at a _____ food restaurant. Let's say you start with $3000, and you add $10 a week to that at a pretty* reasonable rate of _____% a year. In 60 years you'll have $5.6 _____ dollars. That's pretty* amazing, isn't it?

After You Listen

Listen to the conversation again. Each of the following statements about the conversation is incorrect. By changing one word, it is possible to make the statement correct. Find the incorrect word. Change it to the correct word. Be careful. These sentences are paraphrased.

1. Grace thinks most people don't care about saving for the future.

2. It is easy to get information to help plan for your financial future.

3. According to Grace, people need to have two months of salary saved.

4. Baby boomers may have to help their children or their parents.

5. Many common financial emergencies happen expectedly.

6. Younger people are good at saving money.

7. People who can't pay their bills may sell everything.

8. Saving $10 a week is a bad way to start.

9. Thirty percent is a reasonable rate of interest, according to Grace.

10. If you start young enough, it is possible to save billions of dollars before you retire.

Getting Ready to Read

Vocabulary Building

Each of the following words is listed in the newspaper article that you will be reading. You can improve your understanding of this new vocabulary if you first look at these words in context and try to figure out what they mean by identifying synonyms. With a partner,

---

*In colloquial speech, *pretty* is used as a casual synonym for *very*.

This homeless family lives out of their car.

read each of the sentences below. Then examine the synonym list and choose the word that you think would be closest in meaning to the word in **boldface**.

Words from the Article	Synonym List
advocacy	time limit
contends	pride, self-respect
curfew	support
dignity	strict, harsh
evicted	argues
oust	bad situation
plight	thrown out
stringent	kick out

1. Nothing . . . could slap down a working man's **dignity** more than being forced to live in a shelter.

   synonym _____

2. That's what an angry Barker **contends** happened.

   synonym _____

3. The shelter determined the family should be **evicted** because they violated the center's rules.

   synonym _____

4. The San Diego Coalition for the Homeless [is] an **advocacy** group that has tried to help the Barkers find housing.

   synonym _____

5. The shelter threatened to **oust** the family for repeatedly violating rules.

   synonym _____

6. Among the violations was showing a repeated disregard of **curfew** by returning late.

   synonym _____

7. The Barkers' **plight** (1) illustrates problems with . . . **stringent** (2) discipline and eviction policies.

   synonym (1) _____   synonym (2) _____

Read

Family was "Tossed Out" of Shelter, Homeless Man Says

1   Gary Barker thought nothing could get worse. Over the last few months, he lost his job, his car and his home in Oklahoma. As Tulsa became his private dust bowl, he gathered his wife and three children to find a promised land in San Diego.

2   All Barker found here was a homeless shelter. And nothing, Barker figured, could slap down a working man's **dignity** more than being forced to live in a shelter, no matter how pretty and new—like San Diego's famous St. Vincent de Paul–Joan Kroc Center, a peach-colored building at 15th Street and Imperial Avenue.

3   But, Barker said yesterday, he figured wrong. Worse than being in a shelter, Barker observed ruefully, is being "tossed out" of a shelter.

4   And that's what an angry Barker, 31, **contends** happened last Saturday—to himself, his wife, Larissa, 20, and their children, Melissa, 2, Laura, 1, and DeQuion, three months old, at St. Vincent de Paul's.

5   "They threw us out," Barker said. He said the shelter determined that the family should be **evicted** because they violated the center's rules by missing assigned chores and were "uncooperative" with staff.

6   "To come from a middle class background to homelessness is something I didn't realize could happen," Barker said. "And this—

> **Structural unemployment occurs when there are jobs available, and people who want to work, but those looking for jobs can't do the jobs that are available. Rapid changes in technology usually lead to structural unemployment.**

I just couldn't understand it. We didn't deserve this treatment—like animals."

7   "I saw their suitcases come flying out on the sidewalk," recalled Norma Rossi, executive director of the San Diego Coalition for the Homeless, an **advocacy** group that has tried to help the Barkers find housing.

8   "When they called me Saturday, she was crying, and saying 'I can't sleep on the street with a 3-month old baby, what am I going to do?'" said Rossi.

9   St. Vincent de Paul officials yesterday defended their disciplinary practices as necessary to maintain order at the 365-bed shelter. And a high-ranking official there denied that the Barkers were evicted.

10   The Barkers left voluntarily after the shelter threatened to **oust** the family for repeatedly violating rules, said Harvey Mandel, assistant director of St. Vincent de Paul's.

11   "We had a three-page list (of violations)," Mandel said, among them verbal abuse of staff and repeated violations of **curfew.** "It was basic uncooperativeness."

12   "Disciplinary charges against the Barkers had nothing to do with the children," said Mandel.

13   Barker, a college-educated Northern California native, said his troubles started two months ago when he lost his job at an aerospace firm in Oklahoma. After filing for bankruptcy, Barker moved his family to San Diego in hope of gaining another job in the defense industry, where he had worked steadily as a pattern-maker for more than a decade.

14   While seeking work here, Barker and his family spent two weeks at St. Vincent de Paul's center. That's where, Barker said, his "nightmare began."

15   Numerous run-ins between the St. Vincent de Paul staff and the Barkers resulted in eviction threats against his family, Barker acknowledged.

16   In one instance, Barker said St. Vincent's staff refused to provide diapers for his children stricken with diarrhea after the lobby closed for the night.

17   On another occasion, the Barkers contend they were forced to miss their assigned chores because they were spending the day making arrangements for welfare payments.

18   Rossi said the Barkers' **plight** illustrates problems with what she termed St. Vincent's **stringent** discipline and eviction policies.

19   "The shelter's actions are too severe for homeless people already beset with many stress-inducing problems," she said.

20   "It's unjust to put babies out on the street," she said. "Last winter, we had four children and their mother who were put out in the rain. People who are homeless are already under a great deal of stress," she said.

21   Homeless people are routinely asked to leave the St. Vincent de Paul shelter for violating rules.

22   "It happens on a regular basis—but it generally doesn't happen with families," said Mandel of St. Vincent de Paul. "Families usually have a higher regard for their responsibilities."

After You Read

As you read the article, you were probably able to see that the needs of the Barker family were in conflict with the needs of the people who run the shelter. With your partner, complete the grid below. Write statements that describe the needs involved in both sides of this problem.

ACADEMIC POWER STRATEGY

Improve your ability to remember and you will increase your success as a student and a language learner. Students receive a lot of information each day. Remembering it all can be difficult. However, there are some simple things you can do to remember more.

1. As soon as possible, try to *paraphrase* (repeat in your own words) new information.

2. As soon as possible, try to *summarize* (repeat in a shorter form) new information.

3. As soon as possible, copy your class notes to bring the new information to the front of your mind.

Apply the Strategy

In the grid below and on the next page, list and discuss three things that you think the Barker family needs and three things that the shelter officials need. Summarize information from the article to explain.

The Barker Family:	The Shelter Officials:

1. Need:
 	
    Summary:
	1. Need
	
	    Summary:

The Barker Family:	The Shelter Officials:
2. Need: Summary:	3. Need: Summary:
3. Need: Summary:	3. Need: Summary:

Vocabulary Review

Use the new vocabulary you have learned to fill in the blanks in the following dialogue. This dialogue also involves people who have different ideas about following rules and helping those in need.

advocacy   dignity   plight

contend   evicted   stringent (used twice)

curfew   oust

Ms. Dupre: I am here to represent a school _____ group that is working in support of students who have been _____ from the computer laboratory because they were on the computers for too long after the time limit.

Mr. Paulson: Ms. Dupre, we sympathize with your view, but surely you can see how necessary it is for us to have _____ rules when we have so many people who want to use the computer lab. Rules help people to behave with _____ and not act badly.

Ms. Dupre: I do understand, but your rules are too _____. Furthermore, you _____ people from the computer lab as soon as they violate one rule, without giving them a chance to improve their behavior.

Mr. Paulson: I often feel just terrible about treating students in this way, but I have to think about what is best for the largest number of students. I _____ that what's best is to have order and organization for students to rely on when they are try-ing so hard to do well in school.

Ms. Dupre: It is when they are under stress that students need toler-ance. Please, show some sympathy for the _____ these students face. Don't be so hard on them when they break the rules.

Mr. Paulson: Well, maybe we can relax the _____ in the evening to give students more time to work on the comput-ers in the lab when there are fewer people who want to use them.

LANGUAGE YOU CAN USE: DESCRIBING A PROBLEM

DESCRIBING A PROBLEM	EXAMPLE
It seems to me that . . .	*"It seems to me that* the rules should be more flexible."
The real problem is that . . .	*"The real problem is that* some students don't respect the policies of the lab."
It's quite clear that . . .	*"It's quite clear that* the school needs to have rules if everything is to function smoothly."

USING NEW LANGAUGE

With a partner, look at each of the situations described below. You will identify needs and problems that are not economic. Instead, these needs and problems are common among students. Identify the problem that the person in each situation is experiencing. Use the language above to describe problems and to explain what is happen-ing. You and your partner may have different opinions about the problem, which is OK. Just practice using the language.

1. A student has a very difficult time passing examinations, even though she or he participates actively in class and completes home-work assignments. This very busy student has a part-time job and an active social life. Finding blocks of time to study is often difficult.

   What's the problem? _____

   _____

   _____

2. Two roommates are studying in their dormitory room. As they study, they are listening to some music. One roommate keeps changing the station on the radio, looking for a song that he likes. This disturbs the concentration of the second roommate.

What's the problem? _____

_____

_____

3. A student is at the campus computer laboratory waiting to use a computer to finish a homework assignment. All the computers are being used. Some students are using the computers for personal work, not schoolwork.

What's the problem? _____

_____

_____

PART 2: How Can We Offer Help to Others?

LANGUAGE YOU CAN USE: OFFERING ADVICE

OFFERING ADVICE	EXAMPLES
Have you thought about . . .	*"Have you thought about* copying your notes after each class?"
Why don't you . . .	*"Why don't you* check the tutoring board to see if someone can help you with your math class?"
Maybe you could . . .	*"Maybe you could* start a study group and get support from your classmates."
You should/ought to . . .	*"You should/ought to* get a roommate so your rent won't be so expensive."

From the examples, you can see that when we give advice in English we often use **modals** (*could, should, ought to*) and question forms rather than using the imperative (*get a job, get a roommate, sell your car,* etc.). This is to soften the advice and separate giving advice from giving orders. Giving advice is polite and gentle compared to giving orders. Why do you think this might be important?

LANGUAGE YOU CAN USE: DISCUSSING OTHERS' NEEDS

DISCUSSING OTHERS' NEEDS	EXAMPLES
I understand that you . . .	"*I understand that you* think textbooks are very expensive."
It seems to me that you could use . . .	"*It seems to me that you could use* a much better dictionary."
They need . . .	"*They need* a new computer and printer."

 **Getting Ready to Listen**

Work with a partner. Answer the questions below.

1. Do you think it is expensive to get a good education?

2. How much do you know about how college educations are paid for in other countries around the world?

3. Who do you think should cover the cost of college education? Students? Their families? The government?

4. If governments pay for college education for students, should they require these students to earn certain grades? Should they limit the number of students who can attend college?

5. Would you be willing to pay higher taxes throughout your life to make sure everyone who wants a college education can have one?

Despite its recent increase, the minimum wage remains 15% below its average purchasing power in the 1970s, after adjusting for inflation (Kaufman, 1997).

Listen

Listening 2: The Cost of Education

You will hear a conversation between two students. They are talking about the cost of education. The students will use language to *describe a problem*, *offer advice,* and *discuss needs*. As you listen, fill in the blanks with this specific language.

A: I'm really* worried about paying my tuition for the next term at school. School fees are getting so high. I may have to cut back on my classes and work more hours to earn more.

B: _____ worry about that. Every year _____ that more students worry about money.

A: I agree. And it's hard to study full time and hold down any kind of job.

B: _____ applying for financial aid?

A: Ya know, I have, but _____ so many people apply and there's just not enough financial aid available.

B: _____ qualify for some kind of student loan that you would repay after you finish studying. _____ go to the financial aid office and see what the requirements are.

A: I suppose that's true. Sometimes I wish the cost of education were completely covered by the government. It would sure make my life easier.

B: Maybe, but somebody would still be paying for it. Just not you right now. And I sure don't want to pay higher taxes to cover the cost.

A: _____ you just can't give everybody what they want. More services always means more taxes.

B: Don't you think that's true everywhere, and in a lot of different situations? I'm sure we're not the only ones who are worried about this.

A: Oh, I think _____ a lot of people worry about this. And with a good education becoming more and more necessary to get a good job, I think more people will worry in the future. I can't even pay for myself! How am I supposed to save up to pay for my kids to go to school?

B: Hey, when you find the answer to that one, be sure to tell me. You could make a lot of money selling that piece of advice.

*Native English speakers often use *really* to mean *very*.

After You Listen

LANGUAGE LEARNING STRATEGY

Identify the most important words in a sentence by listening for emphasis. When speaking, native speakers often emphasize the words that are most important. By listening for this emphasized intonation, you can hear which ideas the speaker thinks are most important. You can get a better idea of what the speaker wants to communicate. This will improve your understanding.

Apply the Strategy

As you complete "The Sound of It" activity, do the following things:

1. Listen carefully to the tape.

2. For each sentence that you hear from the conversation, circle the word or words that are emphasized.

3. Think about why that word is emphasized. What idea is important to the speaker?

The Sound of It: Meaning from Intonation

1. I'm really worried about paying my tuition for the next term at school. School fees are getting so high.

2. It's hard to study full time and hold down any kind of job.

3. You just can't give everybody what they want.

4. Don't you think that's true everywhere, and in a lot of different situations?

5. I'm sure we're not the only ones who are worried about this.

6. Oh, I think it's quite clear that a lot of people worry about this.

7. I can't even pay for myself! How am I supposed to pay for my kids to go to school?

8. Hey, when you find the answer to that one, be sure to tell me. You could make a lot of money selling that piece of advice.

Now look back at the words you circled. Why do you think the speaker emphasized these words? What is important to the speaker? Compare your ideas with a partner. Write your ideas on the following lines.

1. _____
   _____

2. _____
   _____

3. _____
   _____

4. _____
   _____

5 _____
   _____

6. _____
   _____

7. _____
   _____

8. _____
   _____

Many of the issues and activities in this chapter deal with financial needs. Some people feel comfortable talking about these needs openly, but others think of this subject as something very private. Would you feel comfortable asking for or giving someone advice about a personal financial problem? Write your thoughts in the space below.

_____
_____
_____
_____
_____
_____
_____
_____
_____
_____

LANGUAGE LEARNING STRATEGY

P ractice or repeat new language to make this language become a comfortable, natural part of the English you use everyday. Classroom conversation activities provide excellent opportunities to practice and repeat new language.

Apply the Strategy

As you complete the advice chain activity, do the following things:

1. Make a real effort to use the language presented in the "Language You Can Use" sections (pages 112 and 113).

2. Think about the *meaning* of the language, not just the grammar.

USING NEW LANGUAGE: THE ADVICE CHAIN

You have learned some specific ways to paraphrase someone else's needs and to offer this person advice. Use this language to give your partners advice about the problems listed below. Your teacher will put you into two short lines facing each other. Each person will be given a slip of paper with a problem on it. You will hear about a problem from the person directly across from you. Give that person advice about the problem. You will also explain your problem and receive advice about it. Then you will each move down the line and repeat the exercise, listening to a different problem and giving different advice.

Problem 1: You are a young adult who had a good job, and you have been living on your own for the past couple of years. Recently, you lost your job, and now to have enough money you will probably have to move back home with your parents.

Problem 2: You are taking several classes this semester. In addition, you have a part-time job. It is very difficult for you to find time to study and prepare for all of your classes.

Problem 3: You sit next to a student who often forgets to bring his books, papers, dictionary, etc. to class. This other student always wants to borrow your things and/or look on with you during class. You like this student, but it is distracting to always have to share things during class.

Problem 4: You are taking a class with an exciting teacher. Unfortunately, this teacher talks very quickly and doesn't always write important ideas down on the board. Often, you find it difficult to keep up with what is happening in the class.

Problem 5: You truly enjoy talking with the native English-speaking students on campus, but they use a lot of idioms and slang. Sometimes it is difficult for you to understand them.

Problem 6: You still need a dictionary to help you with new vocabulary when you read in English. Your dictionary is very heavy and takes up a lot of room in your book bag.

Problem 7: Your teacher requires that you type your papers for class on a computer, but you don't have a computer at home and you can't afford to buy or lease one.

Problem 8: You often study with a group of friends who are taking some of the same classes as you are. You like to use this time to discuss what you are doing in class and to work on class assignments. Some of the other students like to talk about non-school subjects. You think this is a waste of time.

Culture Note

It may seem strange to you that living with one's parents is considered a problem, but in some cultures it is quite unusual for grown children to live at home. What happens in your native culture?

TUNING IN:
"Cracking Down on the Homeless"

You will see a CNN video clip about the homeless in San Francisco and Berkeley. Before you watch the clip, talk with a partner and answer these questions.

How do you think neighborhoods are affected when there are many homeless people living in the area?

When you go somewhere and you see a homeless person, how do you feel?

Do you feel comfortable going to that area?

Your instructor will show the video clip several times. Below are some questions about the video. Each question has four answers listed below. Three of the answers are correct. One answer is incorrect. As you listen, circle the answer that is incorrect.

1. What are some of the problems that residents of San Francisco and Berkeley associate with the homeless population?

   a. drugs

   b. prostitution

   c. aggressive behavior

   d. drunkenness

2. When police remove the homeless population, what are some of the benefits the residents see?

   a. The area is cleaner.

   b. Drug dealers are gone.

   c. The area is safer.

   d. The area is friendlier.

3. In order to eliminate public drunkenness, what are some of the strategies used by the police and liquor store owners?

   a. Provide names of homeless people to store owners.

   b. Provide photos of homeless people to store owners.

   c. Refuse to sell alcohol to certain homeless people.

   d. Ask store owners to identify drunken homeless people.

4. Why do advocates for the homeless population feel that there is a recent crackdown on the homeless?

   a. Local government wants to respond to resident complaints about unpopular people in the community.

   b. Governments always crack down on the homeless near election time.

   c. The homeless population has grown a lot recently.

   d. Attitudes towards the homeless run in cycles.

5. What are some of the things police and local governments may do to crack down on the homeless?

   a. Refer to homeless people as criminals.

   b. Make it against the law to be unemployed.

    c. Make it illegal to stay in a public park.

    d. Arrest homeless people for begging, sleeping in public, trespassing, and blocking sidewalks.

Two Views of Homelessness

The CNN video clip shows several different homeless people. How are these people different from Gary Barker and his family? How are they the same? Which view is more stereotypical? Discuss this comparison with a partner.

PUTTING IT ALL TOGETHER

Complete the activities below to measure what you learned while studying from this chapter.

1. Practice your summarizing skills. Write a brief summary of the topics/ideas covered in this chapter.

    _____

    _____

    _____

    _____

    _____

2. A friend comes to you for advice about a personal problem. List one question form and one sentence form you can use to begin the advice you will give.

    Question Form: _____

    _____

    Sentence Form: _____

    _____

3. Your friend studies very hard and is an excellent student. Recently, you have worried that your friend is actually working too hard and worrying too much. Your friend comes to you and talks about feeling very stressed. Articulate/paraphrase your friend's need by completing the three sentences below.

    I understand that you _____

    _____

It seems to me that you could use _____

_____

You need _____

_____

4. What is one thing you have realized about school problems while working through this chapter? Write your answer below.

_____

_____

_____

_____

_____

_____

_____

_____

_____

_____

5. Look at each statement below. Circle your response to the statement. Think about why you chose each response.

   a. I feel confident that I know how to give advice in English.

strongly agree   agree   agree somewhat   disagree   strongly disagree

   b. I know three ways to help me remember new material.

strongly agree   agree   agree somewhat   disagree   strongly disagree

   c. I remember and can use at least four of the new vocabulary words from the reading in this chapter.

strongly agree   agree   agree somewhat   disagree   strongly disagree

   d. I realize that practicing new language I learn will help me improve my English more.

strongly agree   agree   agree somewhat   disagree   strongly disagree

   e. I feel confident that I can correctly use English to identify and talk about problems.

strongly agree   agree   agree somewhat   disagree   strongly disagree

Test-Taking Tip

Improve your performance on multiple choice tests by:

- answering the question in your head before you look at the choices.

- marking questions you can't answer immediately and coming back to them later.

- reading all the answers before selecting one—there may be two that are similar.

CHECK YOUR PROGRESS

On a scale of 1 to 5, rate how well you have mastered the goals set at the beginning of the chapter:

1 2 3 4 5   express needs so you can ask for what is important to you.

1 2 3 4 5   improve your ability to remember.

1 2 3 4 5   offer advice in order to help others get what they need.

1 2 3 4 5   identify the most important words in a sentence by listening for emphasis.

1 2 3 4 5   listen for the language of advice and suggestion so you know when others are trying to help you.

1 2 3 4 5   practice or repeat new language to make the language more familiar and comfortable.

If you've given yourself a 3 or lower on any of these goals:

- visit the *Tapestry* web site for additional practice.

- ask your instructor for extra help.

- review the sections of the chapter that you found difficult.

- work with a partner or study group to further your progress.

The world is becoming increasingly media oriented. For many people, exposure to the media is a common part of daily life.

- How many hours per day do you spend watching television?
- How often do you read a newspaper or news magazine?
- Do you think the electronic and print media have an impact on your thoughts about people and events?

6

I SAID IT MY WAY

In previous chapters, you discussed how you are affected by global and economic issues. Most people are quite interested in these two areas and often seek out information about them. The most common way that people around the world keep themselves informed is through their frequent contact with the mass media, such as newspapers, television, radio, Internet, and magazines. In this chapter, you will examine the media as a source of information and as a cultural influence. How much can you trust the media, and how powerful is their influence over you? Do the media keep you objectively informed, or do they present information to you in a subjective way? These are some of the things you will be thinking about as you examine the modern media.

Setting Goals

In this chapter you will learn how to:

- ◈ recognize the difference between facts and opinions.

- ◈ preface facts and opinions.

- ◈ listen for specific language cues to better understand facts and opinions.

- ◈ prepare effectively for a debate or discussion.

- ◈ relate your learning to the world around you.

Getting Started

Read the statements listed below and decide if you agree or disagree with the statement. Then circle your answer.

What Do I Know About the Topic?

1. I have thought about how the media influence the way I think.   agree   disagree

2. I know what "the right to privacy" means.   agree   disagree

3. I know what I think about people's right to privacy.   agree   disagree

4. I have thought about how watching TV can both help me and harm me.   agree   disagree

5. I read a newspaper or watch TV for information every day.   agree   disagree

What Do I Know About the Language?

1. In my native culture it is acceptable to express your personal opinion.   agree   disagree

2. I am comfortable sharing my opinion in English.   agree   disagree

3. I am comfortable making statements about things I know to be facts.   agree   disagree

4. It is easy for me to know the difference in English between someone telling me an opinion and someone telling me the facts.   agree   disagree

5. I know the different ways that I can express facts and opinions in English.   agree   disagree

In some cultures it is considered rude to express your personal opinion openly, especially about controversial topics. Other cultures consider it necessary and important to share one's views. For example, people in the United States do not consider it rude to express personal opinions freely and openly. How does your native culture feel about this? How do you feel? Why?

PART 1: Television—The Good and the Bad

Ninety-seven percent of the homes in the United States have a color TV.

You probably have many strong ideas about many different topics. You may share these ideas with family, friends, colleagues, or even casual acquaintances. Every day you are also exposed to the opinions of others. Sometimes, hearing others' ideas can influence the way you think about things. Sometimes, you are not even aware of this influence. In the activities that follow, you will examine the difference between sharing an opinion and stating actual facts, and you will look for ways to recognize the difference between fact and opinion when you are exposed to the ideas of other people.

WARMING UP: FACT VS. OPINION— CAN YOU TELL THE DIFFERENCE?

With a partner, look at the statements below. Decide if they are statements of fact or statements of opinion. Then circle your answer. Be prepared to explain your decision.

1. It's well-known that Paris is the capital of France.   fact   opinion

2. I'm positive that emperor penguins can stay under the water for 18 minutes.   fact   opinion

3. In my point of view, Madonna wears very expensive shoes.   fact   opinion

4. It's a fact that blue eyes are more sensitive to light than brown eyes.   fact   opinion

5. I'm positive that left-brained people tend to be more analytical and logical than right-brained people.   fact   opinion

6. I believe that most politicians are dishonest.   fact   opinion

7. I'm absolutely sure that Tokyo is more densely populated than New York.   fact   opinion

8. In my opinion, a little red wine every day never hurt anyone.   fact   opinion

In the space below, list the language that helped you to distinguish fact from opinion.

_____

_____

_____

_____

LANGUAGE YOU CAN USE: STATING FACTS

EXPRESSIONS	EXAMPLES
It's well-known that . . .	*It's well-known that* Madame Curie discovered uranium.
It's a fact that . . .	*It's a fact that* 2 + 2 = 4.
I'm positive that . . .	*I'm positive that* Ronald Reagan was the 36th president of the United States.
I'm (absolutely) sure that . . .	*I'm (absolutely) sure that* Al Pacino starred in *The Godfather*.

The last two are used when you are making a statement that you *believe* to be fact. The information can be checked to see if it is true or false. The first two statements are used when you are stating an absolute fact.

USING NEW LANGUAGE

Practice the language you have learned above to introduce some facts to your classmates. Express some facts that you know by answering the following questions. Then state the facts to a partner.

1. What is a movie that is showing right now?

   _____

2. What is the name of a newspaper you can buy in the area where you live?

   _____

3. What is the name of the current president of the United States?

   _____

4. When was television invented?

_____

LANGUAGE YOU CAN USE: STATING OPINIONS

EXPRESSIONS	EXAMPLES
In my opinion . . .	*In my opinion* tennis is more interesting than soccer.
From my (point of) view . . .	*From my (point of) view* the Doors were the greatest rock group of all time.
I think/believe/feel that . . .	*I think/believe/feel that* we need more women in high-level political positions.

USING NEW LANGUAGE

Use the language you have learned above to state your opinion in response to the questions listed below. Express your opinion to a partner.

1. Who is the greatest popular entertainer in the world today?

   _____

2. What is the most exciting movie you have ever seen?

   _____

3. How much violence is acceptable on television?

   _____

4. How much sexual activity is acceptable in movies?

   _____

People in the United States do not consider it rude to express their personal opinions freely and openly. However, to avoid being too verbally aggressive or being a "know-it-all," they will often *preface* their opinion with the above statements to show that they know that the idea *is* personal and not the only idea. Do you do something similar in your native language?

THE V-CHIP DEBATE

In many homes TV is a baby-sitter for busy parents.

 **Getting Ready to Listen**

Look at the statements below. Decide if you agree or disagree. Circle your answer.

1. I think there is too much sex on TV   agree   disagree

2. I think there is too much violence on TV.   agree   disagree

3. I think sex and violence on TV can be   agree   disagree
   harmful to children.

4. I think parents should do more to   agree   disagree
   control what their kids see on TV.

 Listen   **Listening 1: The V-Chip Debate**

LANGUAGE LEARNING STRATEGY

Listen for specific language cues to better understand conversations in which people express different ideas and opinions. When you learn to recognize the cues, it becomes easier to listen for content.

Apply the Strategy

You will hear a mock debate about the "v-chip," a computer microchip that can be put into a television to prevent certain kinds of programs from being shown. One of the speakers in this debate is a parent who is concerned about what children see on television. The other speaker is an attorney who works to protect people's rights. Listen for the language the speakers use to convey their different opinions. If you need to review the language of opinion, look back at the language box on page 129. As you listen, take notes about the two sides of the debate.

The Parent	The Attorney
_____	_____
_____	_____
_____	_____
_____	_____
_____	_____
_____	_____
_____	_____
_____	_____

After You Listen

Check each of the statements below that paraphrases an idea from the mock debate. If you check the statement, decide whether it was the parent or the attorney who made this statement.

_____ Installing the v-chip is a form of censorship.

   parent   attorney

_____ Parents usually watch TV with their children.

   parent   attorney

_____ People are watching more television.

   parent   attorney

_____ Parents can easily control what their kids watch on television by changing the channel.

   parent   attorney

_____ Choosing what you want to watch is an important personal freedom.

parent   attorney

Now, choose one of the prefaces below and write your own opinion about the use of v-chips.

In my opinion . . . From my point of view . . . I think/believe/feel that . . .

_____

_____

The Mini-Debate

You will each receive one statement to explain and defend in your mini-debate. Take a few minutes to think about the statement and to provide an example that you think illustrates the truth of the statement. Then you will face off against a classmate with an opposing point of view, and you will have a few minutes to convince this person of the truth of your statement. After a short time, the instructor will ask you to change partners, and you will face a new partner with a different, opposing point of view. Be sure to preface your opinion.

LANGUAGE LEARNING STRATEGY

Apply the Strategy

Prepare effectively for a debate or discussion. If you prepare, it is easier to explain your ideas and to persuade others that your idea is right.

Prepare to participate effectively in a debate by doing the following:

1. *Think carefully* about the idea you will present. *Ask yourself* these *questions:* What does this idea really mean? How can I explain it clearly to others?

2. *Look for facts or examples* you can use to support and clarify your idea.

3. *Choose appropriate language* to preface your opinion or show that you are stating a fact you can prove.

Statement 1: Television prevents people from thinking for themselves. It makes people stupid.

Example: _____

_____

Statement 2: Television is the greatest educational tool the world has ever known.

Example: _____

_____

Statement 3: People in contemporary society are often addicted to television.

Example: _____

_____

Statement 4: Watching television is the best way for people to avoid feeling bored and lonely.

Example: _____

_____

Statement 5: Television stimulates the imagination.

Example: _____

_____

Statement 6: Television ruins the imagination.

Example: _____

_____

Statement 7: Television makes it possible for us to have experiences we would never be able to have any other way.

Example: _____

_____

Statement 8: Television makes us spectators of life and not participants in life.

Example: _____

_____

Statement 9: Watching television together is a good way for parents to be close to and spend time with their children.

Example: _____

_____

Statement 10: Television is the world's most dangerous babysitter. It has replaced better activities in which a family could participate together.

Example: _____

_____

Statement 11: Because television gives us a lot of interesting information, it encourages us to share our ideas with other people.

Example: _____

_____

Statement 12: Watching television has, in many cases, replaced real human communication.

Example: _____

_____

CONTROLLING THE INFLUENCE OF TELEVISION

> Television is the first truly democratic culture—the first culture available to everyone and entirely governed by what the people want. The most terrifying thing is what people do want.
>
> —CLIVE BARNES,
> *THE NEW YORK TIMES*

It is estimated that the average person in the United States spends four to six hours a day watching television. The number of television viewing hours is increasing in other countries as well, as economic hard times make it more difficult for many people to go out and pursue other forms of recreation and entertainment. This means that television is now the source from which you draw most of your information, receive entertainment, and form your impressions of the world, events, and people. Something of so much influence should be used with caution and concern. With a group, make four suggestions for how television can be enjoyed responsibly. Think of the needs of adults, children, and families. Remember to use the language for making suggestions and giving advice that you learned in Chapter Five.

Suggestion 1: _____

Suggestion 2: _____

Suggestion 3: _____

Suggestion 4: _____

PART 2: Is This Really News?
··········· The Right to Know vs. the Right to Privacy

Monica Lewinsky under siege by the paparazzi after rumors of her affair with U.S. President Bill Clinton surfaced in the news.

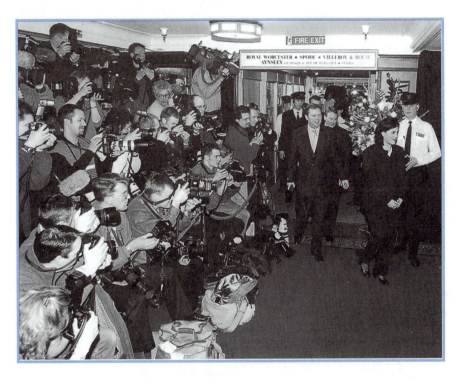

> **A weekly edition of** *The New York Times* **contains more information than the average person was likely to come across in a lifetime in seventeenth-century England.**
>
> **—RICHARD SAUL WURMAN,**
> *INFORMATION ANXIETY*

Often, when you are watching television or involved with the media in other ways, such as reading a newspaper or magazine or listening to the radio, you are learning what is happening in the lives of other people. These people might be politicians, sports figures, or famous actors. Now that the media are so powerful and information is circulated so quickly, the lives of these people are often a matter of public record. They have very little privacy. Sometimes, this is good because it makes it possible for you to know a great deal about the lives and behavior of our political leaders. Sometimes, this information can be harmful to a public figure—for example, if details of their family relationships or health are exposed without their consent. In the next part of the chapter, you will practice sharing your opinions as you discuss which is more important: your right to know certain kinds of information or the right of privacy for individuals.

◆Getting Ready to Read

Vocabulary Building

Below are some vocabulary words from the article. Each word has been defined for you. Read the definitions. Then use the words to fill in the blanks in the sentences.

Definitions

1. peccadilloes (plural noun): mistakes, errors of judgment
2. distressing (adjective): upsetting
3. scrutiny (noun): close examination
4. unprecedented (adjective): never having been done before
5. perjury (noun): the act of lying under oath in a court of law or legal case
6. mainstream (adjective): common, typical, widely accepted by many
7. unsavory (adjective): unappealing, morally distasteful

Sentences

1. To respect her privacy, her friends decided never to talk about the _____ details of her divorce.
2. Among his other _____ was the fact that he lost $5,000 of his parents' money while gambling.
3. Nowadays, politicians face _____ from the press because people are hungry for a lot of information.
4. She was convicted of _____ because she said she filled out her tax forms correctly, but everyone knew she was lying.
5. All the stories about his drug use, drinking, and wild parties contained a lot of _____ details.
6. She doesn't enjoy _____ movies. She prefers unusual movies that most people don't go to see.
7. A woman president in the United States is still _____— but who knows about the future!

Read

A Double Standard or Differing News?

1   Maybe it was better in the old days. You know the old days, don't you? That was a couple of weeks ago, before Kenneth Starr's report on President Clinton was released, when newspapers had no reason to use the front page to examine the sexual peccadilloes of our president in exhausting (and distressing) detail.

2   It's not the first time Clinton's sexual activities have come under public scrutiny or have been the subject of front-page news stories. (Remember Gennifer Flowers and Paula Jones?)* In the past two weeks, however, newspapers have written about the president and Monica Lewinsky in a way that is unprecedented in the history of this country.

3   Even if the issue is perjury, the fact is no one's sex life—the president's or Joe and Jane Citizen's—ever has been reported so fully and in such detail by the mainstream press. The TV analysis I will leave to someone else.

4   Like it or not, the Starr report about matters most people consider private is news because it involves the president of the United States. Journalists have a duty to report the news, however unpleasant or unsavory, especially in the case of the president. Yet, if the man who holds the most powerful office in the nation can be subjected to such detailed examination of matters usually avoided in polite company, does it mean the Union-Tribune** will use its front page to report on the details of the sex lives and practices of other officials?

> The hand that rules the press, the radio, the screen and the far-spread magazine, rules the world.
>
> —JUSTICE WILLIAM BRANDEIS

After You Read

In this editorial, the writer shares her opinion about how much information newspapers printed about the sex life of the president of the United States—Bill Clinton. Answer the questions below about her opinions:

1. In the final paragraph the writer gives reasons to support the opinion that it is right to share private information about the president, and perhaps other public figures. What are these reasons?

2. The writer also expresses concerns about the results of sharing this kind of information. What are her concerns?

3. Do you agree or disagree with the writer's opinion? Do you share her concerns?

*Gennifer Flowers and Paula Jones are other women who claim to have had some kind of sexual encounter or relationship with President Clinton.

**The San Diego Union-Tribune is the newspaper that originally carried this article.

Getting Ready to Listen

How do you feel when you hear or read detailed information about someone's private life in the news? Write about it in the space below. Discuss your response with a partner.

_____

_____

_____

_____

_____

_____

_____

_____

_____

REAL PEOPLE/REAL VOICES

Listen

Listening 2: Bruce's Experience

Bruce is a journalist who has worked for an independent, underground newspaper in San Diego, California. As you listen, read the text. Some words from Bruce's statement have been paired with other, very-similar-sounding words. Listen very carefully. Circle the word Bruce actually says.

Actually, uh, as a journalist I don't think the media/medium should be prying into the private lives/life of public figures, um, especially if those/does actions are not criminal. Obviously, if the public figure has, uh, committed a felony or murdered someone, we, the public should, uh, should know about that. But for extramarital affairs or consensual activities I would say no.

Um, I think the real measure as to weather/whether to publish a story/history or not should be the motivation. In other words, is it being, uh, published solely to increase the sell/sale of newspapers, or enhance the popularity of the journalist? Or is it being published because it's a genuine subject of national interest and concern?

I admit there will be issues where intelligent people, mmm, disagree about which side of this an issue falls/fails on, but other issues will be easier to decide. Maybe a measure can be, if this were to be published about a candidate you support, would you honestly won't/want to go head/ahead with the story?

After You Listen

In every language, people have certain strategies they use to help them get more time when they need to think before speaking. In English, there are several common conversational pauses—noises, words, or sounds that give a speaker time to think before responding in a conversation. Bruce used conversational pauses in the listening activity on page 138. Conversational pauses are most often used if someone is speaking without preparation.

The Sound of It: Conversational Pauses

Listen to the conversational pauses on the tape.

Conversational Pause	Meaning
Uh	I'm thinking. I need time.
Um	I'm thinking. I need time.
Well . . .	I'm thinking. I need time.
Mmm . . .	I don't think I agree.
Hmm . . .	That's interesting. I didn't expect that.

Now listen to the statements below. Listen carefully to the conversational pauses. Decide if the speaker needs time, may not agree, or has heard an interesting, unexpected idea. Check your answer choice on the line provided.

1. Really? Hmm, I read a newspaper every day.

   _____ The speaker needs time to think.

   _____ The speaker may not agree with a previous statement.

   _____ The speaker has heard something unexpected.

2. Mmm, actually, I get a lot of helpful information from using the Internet in the campus computer lab.

   _____ The speaker needs time to think.

   _____ The speaker may not agree with a previous statement.

   _____ The speaker has heard something unexpected.

3. I think, uh, watching television is a pretty good way to improve my English.

_____ The speaker needs time to think.

_____ The speaker may not agree with a previous statement.

_____ The speaker has heard something unexpected.

4. Mmm. We need to have a *lot* more newspapers and magazines available in the library.

_____ The speaker needs time to think.

_____ The speaker may not agree with a previous statement.

_____ The speaker has heard something unexpected.

5. I, um, don't like it that the news on TV shows so much, um, graphic violence nowadays.

_____ The speaker needs time to think.

_____ The speaker may not agree with a previous statement.

_____ The speaker has heard something unexpected.

Discussion

In small groups, answer the following questions.

1. How often do you read or watch the news?

2. Does a society benefit from having citizens who are well informed about what is happening around them? Think of two ways that society might benefit from this.

3. Is it important for the public to know what political and social leaders are doing? Why?

4. Is it important for the public to know what celebrities are doing? Why?

5. What kinds of information do you want to have about politicians? Why?

6. What kinds of information do you want to have about other public figures? Why?

7. What kind of information about politicians and public figures is generally given to the public by the media in your native country?

8. Circle the amount of information you believe you get.

more than enough   enough   not enough

THE RIGHT-TO-PRIVACY SURVEY

A never-ending hunger for news about public figures has created a demand for information that used to be considered very private. It's not even necessary for the news to be factually correct for people to want to read, watch, or hear it.

You are going to take a survey on media issues by talking with one another. To follow are listed some questions related to the issue of privacy. Ask people to answer these questions. Then ask them why they think what they do. After all the class has completed the survey, tally the results on the board to see how your class feels about the right to privacy versus the right to know.

ACADEMIC POWER STRATEGY

Make an effort to see how your learning relates to what is happening in the world around you. A lot of the things you study in school are useful in helping to better understand current events, politics, and people. Your education and your daily life can work together for the benefit of both.

(continued on next page)

Apply the Strategy

As you complete the survey:

1. Think of public figures who are in the news right now.

2. Ask yourself and others if you think the information you are learning about these public figures is something you need to know or is perhaps a violation of privacy.

Outside of class, remember to think about how what you see on TV, read in the newspaper, or hear on the radio may relate to what you study in your classes.

1. Should the names of rape victims be reported by the news media?

   _____ yes   _____ no

   Why?

   _____

2. Should the media tell us if a famous person is homosexual?

   _____ yes   _____ no

   Why?

   _____

3. Should the media tell us if a politician is having personal problems in his or her marriage?

   _____ yes   _____ no

   Why?

   _____

4. Should the media tell us if a politician is having problems with drugs or alcohol?

   _____ yes   _____ no

   Why?

   _____

5. Should the media tell us if a politician is having personal problems with money?

   _____ yes   _____ no

Why?

_____

6. Should the media tell us if a politician has a lover outside of his or her marriage?

_____ yes   _____ no

Why?

_____

7. Do the media have the right to print private information about the family of a politician?

_____ yes   _____ no

Why?

_____

8. Do the media have the right to print private information about famous people such as actors or rock stars?

_____ yes   _____ no

Why?

_____

9. Does a politician's private life tell us anything about how well he or she can do the job?

_____ yes   _____ no

Why?

_____

10. Why do people like to read about the private lives of those who are famous?

We want to see if they are the   _____ yes   _____ no
same as we are.

We feel good when we know they   _____ yes   _____ no
have problems too.

We are just curious and nosy.   _____ yes   _____ no

Other reasons:_____

_____

_____

_____

Don't be surprised if you find out that some of your classmates accept different kinds of behavior from public figures. Culture plays an important part in what you think of as good or bad personal morality. If you are surprised by something, continue to use the Language Learning Strategy of asking questions to gather information so that you can learn more about this part of your classmates' cultures.

TUNING IN:
"Do We Really Need to Know?"

© CNN

You will see the opening section of a program called *Crossfire*. On this program, people debate current events and issues. Before you watch the clip, talk with a partner and answer these questions.

> What kind of information do you think people truly need to know about politicians before they vote?
> Have you ever refused to vote for someone because of something you learned about his or her personal life?

The topic of this excerpt is whether or not the press should reveal private information about politicians. As you listen, circle the correct answers to the question about the remarks by Pat Buchanan, one of the commentators on *Crossfire*.

1. Why does reporter Jennet Conant feel that the story she wrote about a politician and his marriage was something people should know about?

   a) because it is important for politicians to be happily married

   b) because the politician was powerful and popular, and the story had been around for years without becoming public knowledge

   c) because the politician lied about his marriage

2. What does Mayor Giuliani think people should do with Jennet Conant's article?

   a) read it carefully and try to decide if it is true

   b) ignore it because the article is unfair

   c) throw it in the trash

3. Who are the two political figures mentioned in this program?

    a) the mayor of New York City and the governor of New York

    b) the governor of New York City and the president of the United States

    c) the mayor of New York City and the president of the United States

4. What does the story about Rudy Giuliani allege (claim is true)?

    a) that he has been having an affair for three years and his wife plans to leave him

    b) that he has had affairs with a lot of women

    c) that his wife is having an affair and plans to leave him

5. Which two magazines are mentioned?

    a) *Vanity Fair* and *Time*

    b) *Time* and *Newsweek*

    c) *Vanity Fair* and *Newsweek*

CRITICAL THINKING/DISCUSSION

In this chapter, you have read an article and heard an excerpt from a program about the conflict between the "right to know" and the "right to privacy" of public figures. Work with a partner. Discuss the questions below.

1. Why do you think the media keep revealing private information about public figures even though some journalists are not sure this the right thing to do?

2. Imagine that you are journalists. Give your opinion about why is it necessary and/or important to reveal private information about public figures.

3. Imagine that you are politicians. Give your opinion about why private information should remain private.

PUTTING IT ALL TOGETHER

Look at the following statements. Decide if the statement is a fact or an opinion. Then choose an appropriate preface.

1. _____ Leonardo DiCaprio starred in the movie *Titanic*.

2. _____ *Titanic* is an excellent movie.

3. _____ There is too much violence in films today.

4. _____ We know more about public figures than we used to.

5. _____ A TOEFL score of 550 is required to attend that university.

Complete the statements below to review some of what you learned in this chapter.

1. When talking with native speakers, I will feel more comfortable expressing my own opinion because . . .

   _____

2. One thing that I learned that surprised me about what is expected from public figures in another country was . . .

   _____

3. When I want to distinguish between what I know and what I think, I will do so by saying . . .

   _____

4. If I need more time to think when I am speaking, I can . . .

   _____

Test-Taking Tip

When you have no idea of the answer to a multiple choice test, use these techniques:

- If two answers are similar except for one or two words, choose one of these.
- If two answers have similar sounding/looking words, choose one of these.
- Eliminate grammatically incorrect answers.
- If two quantities are almost the same, choose one of these.

CHECKING YOUR PROGRESS

On a scale of 1 to 5, rate how well you have mastered the goals set at the beginning of the chapter:

1 2 3 4 5   recognize the difference between facts and opinions.

1 2 3 4 5   preface facts and opinions.

1 2 3 4 5   listen for specific language cues to better understand facts and opinions.

1 2 3 4 5   prepare effectively for a debate or discussion.

1 2 3 4 5   relate your learning to the world around you.

If you've given yourself a 3 or lower on any of these goals:

- visit the *Tapestry* web site for additional practice.
- ask your instructor for extra help.
- review the sections of the chapter that you found difficult.
- work with a partner or study group to further your progress.

Socrates and Buddha—two of the most influential minds in history

Everyone has values that are important in helping decide how to conduct daily life.

- What are five values that you learned growing up?
- Where did you learn these values? How were the values taught to you?
- Do you try to live according to these values in your daily life?

IT'S NOT EASY BEING GOOD

In previous chapters, you discussed the importance of resolving conflict through negotiation in situations involving different countries, people in different economic situations, even problems between the genders. You have also seen how the media can influence people in many of these areas, perhaps even affecting how relationships between individuals and nations are negotiated. In everyday life, your willingness to negotiate may often be based on what you can gain from helping or working with others. In this chapter, you will explore your connections to other people, be they family, friends, or members of your community, and your own sense of personal responsibility to these people.

Setting Goals

In this chapter you will learn how to:

◈ improve your pronunciation by listening carefully and imitating native speakers.

◈ talk about hypothetical situations.

◈ use new language as soon as you learn it to remember it better.

◈ respond nonjudgmentally.

◈ search for ideas that challenge your own.

149

**Getting Started**

What Do I Know About the Topic?

Using a scale of 1–5 (1 being the most important, 5 being the least important), rank the following in order of importance. Use each number only once.

1. _____ Your responsibility to yourself.

   _____ Your responsibility to your family.

   _____ Your responsibility to your girlfriend/boyfriend or husband/wife.

   _____ Your responsibility to your community.

   _____ Your responsibility to your friends.

2. Why did you rank each of these as you did?

3. What is more important, being good or being happy?

What Do I Know About the Language?

Respond to each of the statements below using T for **true** or F for **false**.

1. _____ I know what a hypothetical situation is.

2. _____ I have studied and I understand modal auxiliaries.

3. _____ I have studied and I understand conditional verb tenses.

4. _____ I know how to respond politely in English when someone says something that shocks or surprises me.

5. _____ I know how to ask appropriate questions in English so that I can learn more about difficult or controversial topics.

6. _____ I feel comfortable speaking in English about difficult or controversial topics.

> **Morality is largely a matter of geography.**
>
> —ELBERT HUBBARD

RANKING ACTIVITY

1. Individually rank the following values according to how important they are to you. Again, use a scale of 1–5 (1 being the most important, 5 being the least important). You may use each number as many times as you wish.

_____ honesty	_____ tolerance
_____ generosity	_____ compassion
_____ discretion	_____ self-discipline
_____ loyalty	_____ conviction
_____ fidelity	_____ commitment

2. Compare your answers with a partner or in a small group. Answer these questions: Do you feel the same way about certain values, or do you feel differently? Did many of you rank the same values as most/least important?

Different people may place different levels of importance on certain values or personal behaviors. The meaning of words like _honesty_ and _commitment_ may vary from person to person and culture to culture. What influenced your values? What are some values that are particularly important to you that may be less important for your classmates? Discuss this with another student.

PART 1: Thinking About What Is Right

Getting Ready to Read

Vocabulary Building

Read the sentences below. Each sentence contains a vocabulary word that you will hear on the tape and read in the reading. Try to understand the words in the context of the sentence.

1. The teen-age years can be a difficult **transition** between childhood and adulthood.

2. After Kristoffer ran five miles, all his energy was **spent.**

3. A _B+_ is a very **creditable** grade. I hope you feel proud.

4. Fatima's sense of humor is her most noticeable **trait.**

5. Cigarette smoking is **proscribed** on airplane flights.

6. No, Maria is not one of my **contemporaries.** She is actually many years younger than I am.

7. After Grace stayed out in the rain, she **succumbed** to a terrible cold.

8. After she lost her job and failed the test, she felt real **despair.**

9. It was such a beautiful summer day that Tomás decided to go for a long, **aimless** walk on the beach after he finished his homework.

Now match the vocabulary word in Column A with the synonym or definition in Column B.

Column A	Column B
_____ 1. transition	a. characteristic
_____ 2. spent	b. without purpose or direction
_____ 3. creditable	c. prohibited, forbidden
_____ 4. trait	d. change
_____ 5. proscribed	e. respectable, admirable
_____ 6. contemporaries	f. used up
_____ 7. succumbed	g. peers
_____ 8. despair	h. sadness, depression
_____ 9. aimless	i. gave in

Read

We live in a transition period, when the old faiths which comforted nations, and not only so, but made nations, seem to have spent their force. I do not find the religions of men at this moment very creditable to them. . . . The fatal trait is the divorce between religion and morality. Here are know-nothing religions or churches that proscribe intellect . . . the lover of the old religion complains that our contemporaries, scholars as well as merchants, succumb to a great despair . . . and believe in nothing. In our large cities, the population is godless . . . no bond, no fellow-feeling, no enthusiasm. There are not men, but hungers, thirsts, fevers, and appetites walking. How is it people manage to live on—so aimless as they are?

—Ralph Waldo Emerson

After You Read

Work with a partner. Answer the following questions about the reading.

1. Ralph Waldo Emerson says that "We live in a transition period," but he wrote this essay over 100 years ago. Do you think we are also living in a transition period now? What is the transition we are experiencing?

2. In your opinion, what is the difference between "religion" and "morality"? Do you agree with Emerson that there is now separation between religion and morality?

3. Do you live in a large city or in a smaller town? Do you think Emerson is correct when he says there is no "fellow-feeling" in large cities? What do you think he means? Is there fellow-feeling in smaller towns, in your opinion?

4. Do you think Emerson had a positive or negative view of people and ethics? Do you think he is correct? Explain your answer.

The Sound of It: Stress Placement

Listen to the tape. You will hear the passage you just read. First, listen for the vocabulary words you learned. As you listen, note the syllable where the correct stress is placed.

LANGUAGE LEARNING STRATEGY

Improve your pronunciation by listening carefully and imitating native speakers. By listening to and imitating native speakers, you learn to hear and repeat words correctly. Think about these questions.

1. How does a native speaker say the word?

2. Where does a native speaker place the stress?

Apply the Strategy

Let your ears help you get useful information about speaking correctly. In the next exercise,

1. Listen carefully.

2. Repeat exactly what you hear.

3. Check the stressed syllable on the page.

1. transition   ———— 1st   ———— 2nd   ———— 3rd

2. creditable   ———— 1st   ———— 2nd   ———— 3rd

3. proscribe   ———— 1st   ———— 2nd   ———— 3rd

4. contemporaries   ———— 1st   ———— 2nd   ———— 3rd

5. succumbed   ———— 1st   ———— 2nd   ———— 3rd

6. despair   ———— 1st   ———— 2nd   ———— 3rd

7. aimless   ———— 1st   ———— 2nd   ———— 3rd

Continue to *apply the strategy*. Listen and repeat other words from the reading. Check the stressed syllable.

8. divorce   ———— 1st   ———— 2nd   ———— 3rd

9. morality   ———— 1st   ———— 2nd   ———— 3rd

10. complain   ———— 1st   ———— 2nd   ———— 3rd

11. enthusiasm   ———— 1st   ———— 2nd   ———— 3rd

12. population   ———— 1st   ———— 2nd   ———— 3rd

13. comforted   ———— 1st   ———— 2nd   ———— 3rd

14. nations   ———— 1st   ———— 2nd   ———— 3rd

15. fatal   ———— 1st   ———— 2nd   ———— 3rd

16. intellect   ———— 1st   ———— 2nd   ———— 3rd

17. scholars   ———— 1st   ———— 2nd   ———— 3rd

18. merchants   ———— 1st   ———— 2nd   ———— 3rd

19. nothing   ———— 1st   ———— 2nd   ———— 3rd

20. godless   ———— 1st   ———— 2nd   ———— 3rd

21. hunger   ———— 1st   ———— 2nd   ———— 3rd

22. fever   ———— 1st   ———— 2nd   ———— 3rd

23. appetite   ———— 1st   ———— 2nd   ———— 3rd

As you can see, many common English words have the stress on the first or second syllable. It is more unusual to find the stress on the third syllable. None of the words you heard had the stress on the fourth syllable. Remembering this can help you to pronounce new words in English correctly.

PART 2: Exploring Ethics

Write About It.

Think of a time in the past when it was very difficult for you to decide the right thing to do. What did you worry about when you made your decision? Did other people you care about agree or disagree with your decision? How did you feel?

_____

_____

_____

_____

_____

REAL PEOPLE/REAL VOICES

On the tape you will hear a man talking about his own experiences thinking about ethics and values in modern life.

Getting Ready to Listen

In this chapter, you are learning about ethics, about what good behavior is. Chris will talk about this. Before you listen, write down your answers to the questions below.

What do you think it means to be a good person?

_____

> So far, about morals, I know only that what is moral is what you feel good after and what is immoral is what you feel bad after.
>
> —ERNEST HEMINGWAY

What are two personality traits/characteristics you think a good person has?

_____

What are two things you think a good person does when he or she talks to other people?

_____

Listen

Listening 1: Chris's Experience

Read the following transcript of the tape. There are 15 errors in the transcript. Listen carefully to the tape. Listen for what Chris says. Correct the errors.

Chris's Experience

When I was a small boy, the motto of our school was "Do It If It's Right," and what I have been doing since then, that motto has been lingering with me; I was looking for a philosophical and a spiritual framework that included these ethics without getting hung up in a dogma of worshipping a divine figure. I could never buy into a Christian idea of a divine spirit that would judge our foibles and our failures and our successes. I have always believed that those judgments were best left to the individual and that there was always a choice for redemption, not from some higher figure but actually from our own actions. Buddhism is one philosophy and practice that helps me to beware of my own failures and helps me to be aware of how to re-, continually repeat and continually address, you know, mistakes I might make in treating other people. It also helps me understand the idea of causation and how my actions affect others, and how a single action from one individual will affect another individual's reaction, and that brings home the importance of having correct speech, correct actions, correct intonations, and correct wisdom in dealing with situations and with older people. I think it's very important to deal with people and give them toys and hope and confidence and compassion in every circumstance because that helps carry them alone and helps make the word in a very small way a much better place. I can always be a better person, and Buddhism helps me reflect on that so I can be a better person. It shows me that my comprehension for other human beings can be without limits, and the only limits that exist are ones that I set myself. And it always, it goes back to that motto that stuck in me to "Do It Because It's Right," and if I have a framework where I can check my acts and check my intentions and check how I behave with other people, I can always make sure that I do it because it's right, and that's why I am an avid practitioner.

Buddhism is becoming more popular in many countries around the world. The Dali Lama is the leader of Tibetan Buddhism.

◆**After You Listen**   With a partner, discuss the questions below about Chris and his experience.

1. What country do you think Chris is from? Does it surprise you that he is interested in Buddhism? Why or why not?

2. The motto of Chris's school was "Do It Because It's Right." What do you think this means? Do you agree?

3. Chris says that for him, Buddhism is a philosophy, not a religion. What do you think he means by this?

4. According to Chris, how do people's actions affect other people?

5. What does Chris want to give to people? How does he want to treat them?

6. Compare what Chris says with your answers from "Getting Ready to Listen." Do you think Chris is a good person? Why or why not?

LANGUAGE YOU CAN USE: TALKING ABOUT HYPOTHETICAL SITUATIONS

EXPRESSIONS	EXAMPLES
Well, one thing I might do is . . .	*Well, one thing I might do is* admit my mistake.
If I . . ., I would . . .	*If I* saw someone drop $10, *I would* tell them.
I would never even consider. . .	*I would never even consider* lying.
It's possible that I would . . .	*It's possible that I would* lie about my age.
It's inconceivable to me that anyone could . . .	*It's inconceivable to me that anyone could* cheat on his or her taxes.

USING NEW LANGUAGE

LANGUAGE LEARNING STRATEGY

Use new words, phrases, and expressions as soon as you learn them. Use them as soon as you can so that you don't forget their meaning and how they are used. Following are some ways to quickly use new language:

(continued on next page)

1. Write a sentence or two using the new language.

2. Look for an opportunity to use the new language in conversation.

3. Include the new language in a classroom or homework assignment.

Look for every opportunity to use new language that you learn. Soon the language will be a natural, comfortable part of your English.

Apply the Strategy

In the "warming up" activity, you shared some values that are important to you. Now think about applying these values to the following situations as you describe what you would do in each of them. Use the language you have just learned to do so. Listen and respond to others during the activity as you want them to listen and respond to you.

> It is our responsibilities, not ourselves, that we should take seriously.
>
> **—PETER USTINOV**

1. You are in love with the man who sells you pizza in the school cafeteria. Recently, he has not been charging you for the pizza. What would you do?

2. At the movies on Saturday you saw one of your teachers on a date with another student. What would you do?

3. You have an elderly parent who is no longer strong enough to live alone. What would you do?

4. You are unable to have children. A child is available to adopt right now. However, this child is of a different race than you and your spouse. What would you do?

5. A student in your class is asking the teacher if he can make up a test because he was ill. The day of the test, you saw this student. He was not ill. What would you do?

6. You and your friends are sitting in a cafe. They start criticizing the character of someone you know. You know their information is untrue, but you don't want to alienate your friends. What would you do?

7. You have been married for a few years, and it is not working out the way you had hoped. You are very unhappy and do not think the marriage will ever offer you any happiness at all. What would you do?

8. You are failing your writing class and know that you cannot complete your final project on time. You find out that on your campus there are some students who are willing to sell papers they have written in the past. What would you do?

This biracial couple is raising their adopted children, who are also of different races, as one big loving family.

LANGUAGE YOU CAN USE: NONJUDGMENTAL RESPONDING

EXPRESSIONS	EXAMPLES
Well, that's an interesting way to . . .	*Well, that's an interesting way to* deal with criminals.
Hmm, I never thought of . . .	*Hmm, I never thought of* outlawing divorce to keep families together.
Isn't it difficult to . . .	*Isn't it difficult to* have so many family members together in one house?

USING NEW LANGUAGE: CROSS-CULTURAL DISCUSSION

Practice responding nonjudgmentally to ideas that may challenge your own. With a partner, look again at the situations from the values-clarification activity. Talk about your different answers to the question "What Would You Do?"

EXAMPLE: A: If my teacher were dating another student, I would talk to him and tell him that I think that is bad behavior.

B: Isn't it difficult to get in the middle of other people's relationships?

ACADEMIC POWER STRATEGY

Apply the Strategy

Search for ideas that challenge your own. Actively look for new and different ideas. New ideas push you to grow and learn. New ideas provide opportunities for you to use language and develop your mind. They help you see the world outside your own life.

Choose one or two of the following places where you can find many new ideas to think and talk about.

1. Go to the campus library. Read a magazine (in English, of course) that you don't normally read.

2. Join a campus club or organization that works for a cause, like the environment or helping students register to vote.

3. Read the campus newspaper. See what students and teachers on your campus are thinking about.

4. Don't be afraid of conversations where you disagree with people about issues or experiences. These conversations are opportunities to learn and to practice responding politely and appropriately.

Often, when you discuss things like values and standards of personal behavior, it is difficult to be tolerant of how different people deal with these very emotional, subjective topics. It is easy to judge something that is **"different"** and decide that it is **"bad."** Of course, **"different" is just that—different, not good or bad.** As you do the next activity, you may be shocked or surprised by things that you hear. Be extra sensitive to things you say that may be shocking to others . . . you just might learn a lot!

LISTEN FOR THE LANGUAGE

Listen to the taped conversation about some ethical problems that the individuals on the tape are experiencing. After you have listened, use the learning strategy of summarizing to write down the views that are expressed about each specific problem.

◆ **Getting Ready to Listen**

In this exercise you will listen for the language people use to respond nonjudgmentally and to see both sides of an issue. Review the language boxes on pages 157 and 159. On the lines below, write down some of the expressions. This will help you remember the language to listen for.

1. _____

2. _____

3. _____

4. _____

5. _____

◆ **Listen**

Listening 2: Listening for the Language

This is another opportunity to practice summarizing and paraphrasing as you respond to what you hear on the tape. Use these skills to describe the two sides of the problem that the people on the tape are having.

Dialogue 1: Alternative Pain Medicine

1. What is the ethical problem these people are having?

   _____

2. What are the two sides of this issue?

   Side one: _____

   Side two: _____

3. What language do you hear these people use as they discuss the topic? Write down the examples you hear of talking about hypothetical situations and responding nonjudgmentally.

   Talking about hypothetical situations:

   _____

   _____

Responding nonjudgmentally:

_____

_____

When family members do not live close together, or when an elderly person has special medical needs, it may become necessary to place that person in a facility for senior citizens.

Dialogue 2: What's Best for Grandmother

1. What is the ethical problem these people are having?

   _____

2. What are the two sides of this issue?

   Side one: _____

   Side two: _____

3. What language do you hear these people use as they discuss the topic? Write down the examples you hear of talking about hypothetical situations and responding nonjudgmentally.

Talking about hypothetical situations:

_____

_____

_____

Responding nonjudgmentally:

_____

_____

_____

◆After You Listen

Compare your notes with a classmate. Then discuss your answers to the questions below. As you discuss your answers, continue to use the language of nonjudgmental responding and talking about hypothetical situations.

1. What do you think of the alternative pain medicine? Would you try this?

2. Do you think the doctor is right to suggest this alternative to a patient?

3. Would you consider placing an elderly relative in a nursing home? Why or why not?

TUNING IN: "Teaching Character"

You will see a video clip about an elementary school that has begun a program to teach character to children. Before you watch the clip, talk with a partner and answer these questions.

> How can teachers in elementary school teach character and values to children?
> Should teachers teach character and values?

Error Correction

Below are seven statements about what you will hear on the video. Each statement has one error. Correct the errors as you watch and listen.

1. The school in this video is located in Dayton, Idaho.

2. When Rudy Bernardo first became principal of the school, some of the kids came to school on drugs.

3. Character and values include honesty, responsibility, integrity, and humor.

4. Parents compiled a list of character values. They call these the words of the week.

5. The elected school board is against character education.

6. Test scores have fallen at the school since the program of character education began.

7. Schools in at least five other states have adopted a similar program of character education.

© CNN

Listening for Concepts

Watch the video clip again. As you watch, listen for the answers to these questions.

1. Does Rudy Bernardo think children can learn reading, writing, and arithmetic if they don't have good values and discipline?

2. According to the video, why do schools need to teach values to children?

In Your Own Words

With a partner, briefly discuss the video. What is the main point of the video? Would you want your children to participate in a program of character education? Do you agree that parents are no longer as able to teach values at home? Why do you think this could be true?

PUTTING IT ALL TOGETHER

Complete the following sentences.

1. The next time I want to talk about something I might possibly do, I will say . . .

2. I would never even consider . . .

3. It's inconceivable to me that anyone could . . .

Answer the questions below. Use the language you learned in this chapter.

1. What are two questions you can ask someone who says something that shocks or surprises you?

2. What are two statements you can make to someone who says something that shocks or surprises you?

Make a list of four times during the week when you have the opportunity to listen carefully to and imitate native speakers. Then use a scale of 1–5 (1 for very likely, 5 for very unlikely), and decide how likely you would be to practice the strategy in this situation.

_____

_____

On the lines below, write down two things you can do in the next week to find new ideas that will challenge your own (for example, reading a new magazine).

_____

_____

Test-Taking Tip

Improve your performance on True/False tests by using these techniques:

- Read carefully—sometimes one word can make an answer inaccurate.
- Look for qualifiers—*all, most, sometimes, never, rarely* are key words.
- If the question contains the words *always* or *never,* it is usually false.

CHECK YOUR PROGRESS

On a scale of 1 to 5, rate how well you have mastered the goals set at the beginning of the chapter:

1 2 3 4 5   improve your pronunciation by listening carefully and imitating native speakers.

1 2 3 4 5   talk about hypothetical situations.

1 2 3 4 5   use new language as soon as you learn it to remember it better.

1 2 3 4 5   respond nonjudgmentally.

1 2 3 4 5   search for ideas that challenge your own.

If you've given yourself a 3 or lower on any of these goals:

- visit the *Tapestry* web site for additional practice.
- ask your instructor for extra help.
- review the sections of the chapter that you found difficult.
- work with a partner or study group to further your progress.

Advancements in technology make it possible for people to do many things for themselves that were impossible in the past. This woman is checking the results of a home pregnancy test.

Progress in science and technology can make life easier. Can this progress also make life more difficult?

8

SCIENTIFICALLY SPEAKING

In the preceding chapter, you examined your personal values and the impact of those values on your decision making and behavior. One area in which people today are frequently finding their values challenged is science and technology. As more and more past dreams become present realities, you are confronted with choices about right and wrong that past generations never had to consider. You question whether or not to put limits on science and technology, how these things should be used, and who should control them if they are to be controlled at all. In this chapter, you will be applying your value system to the specific area of science and technology.

Setting Goals

In this chapter you will learn how to:

◈ express both sides of an issue.

◈ recognize different points of view.

◈ express compromise.

◈ analyze the meaning of a new word by relating it to something familiar.

◈ understand whole ideas rather than individual vocabulary words.

◈ talk about uncomfortable subjects with greater comfort and confidence.

Getting Started

What Do I Know About the Topic?

1. You are now going to do a "quick write." This is an opportunity for you to think in writing in order to discover ideas you have about a certain topic. You will write for ten minutes about the following question. Write whatever comes into your mind, and do not stop writing for those ten minutes. Do not be concerned with grammar, punctuation, or the correctness of your language. Just use this time to get your ideas down on paper.

Question: Is it possible for science and technology to go too far? Should there be limits on progress, or should scientists always try to learn and do more?

_____

_____

_____

_____

_____

_____

2. With a partner, share the most important ideas from your quick write.

What Do I Know About the Language?

1. When I feel that someone is overlooking one side of an issue, I usually say . . .

_____

2. When I only partly agree with someone, I usually say . . .

_____

3. When I want to show someone that I understand his or her point of view, I . . .

_____

4. I understand and can explain what a compromise is. A compromise is . . .

_____

5. When I am willing to compromise with someone whose ideas are different from my own, I . . .

_____

Warming Up

With a partner, list at least five ways you use science and technology in your daily life.

A person on the moon weighs 1/6 of his or her weight on Earth.

1. _____

2. _____

3. _____

4. _____

5. _____

PART 1: Progress, Progress, Progress!

LANGUAGE YOU CAN USE: EXPRESSING DIFFERENT VIEWPOINTS

SEEING BOTH SIDES	EXAMPLES
On one hand . . . on the other hand . . .	*On one hand,* this invention will save many lives . . . *On the other hand,* it produces a lot of waste.
One way of looking at it is . . . **Another way of looking at it is . . .**	*One way of looking at it is* science is our future. *Another way of looking at it is* science could be the end of us.
Yes, but the flip side of the issue is . . .	Of course, nuclear power produces a lot of energy, *but the flip side of the issue is* that it can be very dangerous.
Well, scientifically speaking . . .	*Well, scientifically speaking,* cosmetic surgery is low risk.
You can't ignore . . .	*You can't ignore* the positive value of genetic engineering.

EXPRESSING COMPROMISE	EXAMPLES
I see your point, but . . .	*I see your point, but* in the wrong hands this technology could be dangerous.
Maybe you have a point there . . .	*Maybe you have a point there.* We could eliminate some testing of cosmetics on animals.
Yes, I suppose you could say . . .	*Yes, I suppose you could say* computers increase productivity even though they dehumanize the workplace.
I guess you're right, although . . .	*I guess you're right* and I should write letters by hand, *although* I still think using the computer is a lot more convenient.

Culture Note

The previous "Language You Can Use" activity uses the verb *see* in a way that is different from what we normally mean when we use this word. The word *see* is easy to understand, but it can mean more than seeing with the eyes. What are some other ways to interpret the word *see*? How do these other meanings help to understand the expression *seeing both sides*? In English the verb *to see* is used to mean *to understand*. This demonstrates in the most direct way possible that a speaker recognizes and fully comprehends what another person is saying even if the speaker doesn't agree. Native speakers also say, "It's important to see the other side" or "I see both sides of the issue." This is done to show that the speaker recognizes that there are other viewpoints just as valid as his or her own. This makes it possible to disagree without saying that the other person is wrong. In your native culture, what do you say when you disagree with someone? Can you accept this point of view as well as your own, or is it necessary to make the other person wrong so that you can be right?

The Sound of It: Using Intonation to Emphasize Different Points of View

In conversation, people often want to make it clear that while they see the other person's point of view, they have a different point of view. Or they may want to show that they are willing to compromise, but they don't agree completely. One way to do this is to emphasize certain words as the speaker paraphrases the different ideas. Listen to the tape. Circle which words are emphasized. Underline the different points of view.

1. On the one hand, it is important to test products for safety before selling them, but on the other hand, you can't deny that many animals have to suffer terribly in order for these products to be tested.

2. One way of looking at it is to say technology can be very dangerous, but another way of looking at it is to recognize that the technology is neutral. It's people who make it dangerous when they use it in harmful ways.

3. Yes, I supposed you could say that e-mail saves a lot of time at work. You could also say that communication through computers eliminates important human contact that builds important relationships.

4. I guess you're right that computers are very helpful and useful for students, but you can't ignore that some students spend so much time on their computers that they don't develop other necessary life skills.

> Ours is a world of nuclear giants and ethical infants. We know more about war than we know about peace, more about killing than we know about living. We have grasped the mystery of the atom and rejected the Sermon on the Mount.
>
> **—GENERAL OMAR N. BRADLEY**

USING NEW LANGUAGE

As we keep moving forward through research and experimentation, we must confront certain ethical questions. What are our rights as opposed to the rights of our environment and the other creatures who share it with us?

In each of the situations below, both choices have good points and bad points. With a partner, discuss these situations and what you would choose to do in them. Have each partner take one side of the issue. Use the language of "seeing both sides" and "expressing compromise" as you discuss. Be sure to use correct intonation when you see both sides and express compromise.

1. If you find a large insect in your kitchen, it is better to (take the insect outside) (use an insecticide spray to kill the insect).

2. When you are ill, you should (see a doctor immediately to get a prescription medicine) (use familiar home remedies made with natural ingredients like tea and lemon).

3. When you need to discuss a problem with a business colleague, it is better to initiate contact (in person) (through writing).

4. When you are angry, it is better to (express yourself immediately) (contain your anger until you feel calm).

5. When you don't know the answer to a question on a test, it is better to (guess) (think carefully about what you do know and see if this knowledge can help you on the test).

TECHNOLOGY VS. MORALITY

LANGUAGE LEARNING STRATEGY

Relate the meaning of a new word or phrase to something that is familiar to you. This makes it easier to understand specific vocabulary and to see relationships between words and ideas. Sometimes, you can clarify your understanding of a word by making associations with other words that you already know, and these words give you a clearer picture of the new, difficult vocabulary.

Apply the Strategy

Work together with your classmates to list synonyms that define the following two words. On the next page, list your synonyms in the spaces below each word.

Light travels at 186,000 miles per second.

Activity 1: Associating

TECHNOLOGY	MORALITY
progress	ethics

Activity 2: Values Clarification

Look at the technologies listed below. Individually, decide whether each one is **good, bad,** or **neutral.** Check the appropriate box.

Technology	Good	Bad	Neutral
computers			
euthanasia			
abortion			
birth control			
cloning			
animal experimentation			
video games			
nuclear power			
genetic engineering			
animal transplants			

Often, cultural background can have a strong influence on how people perceive even the most technical or practical aspects of life. Does your native culture have any specific values or beliefs that influence the way you think about the examples of technology that are listed on the previous page?

Discussion

Work in small groups and compare your checklist from page 172 with those of your group members. As you do this, practice the language that has been presented to encourage everyone to share different viewpoints. Make compromises if possible. Look back at the box on page 169 to review the language if necessary.

EXAMPLE: Student A: I think microwave ovens are bad because they emit harmful rays that can cause cancer.

Student B: *Yes, but you can't ignore the fact* that they save working people a lot of time.

Student A: *Mmmmm . . . you have a point there*, but I think the dangers of cancer outweigh the convenience of saving time.

SEEING BOTH SIDES: THE RADIO DEBATE

◆**Getting Ready to Listen**

You will hear a simulated radio talk show about a controversial and perhaps painful subject. Before you listen, read each of the statements below. Decide if you agree or disagree. Be prepared to explain why you feel this way.

1. The primary responsibility of doctors is to prevent and eliminate human suffering.

    agree   disagree

2. The primary responsibility of doctors is to preserve every single human life.

    agree   disagree

3. Religion and science are separate and should be kept separate.

    agree   disagree

4. If one person suffers to help many, it is worth it.

agree   disagree

 Listen

Listening 1: Seeing Both Sides

Listen to the following simulated radio talk show, which is on the topic of using human fetal tissue for medical experimentation. A debate takes place between a leading scientist and a religious leader. As you listen the first time, try to answer the following questions.

1. What is Dr. Benson's main point? _____

_____

2. What is Reverend Cooper's main point? _____

_____

As you listen a second time, list the arguments that each of the speakers uses to support his or her main point.

Dr. Benson: Arguments in favor of fetal tissue use

_____

_____

_____

Reverend Cooper: Arguments against fetal tissue use

_____

_____

_____

 **After You Listen**

After you listen a third time, write two expressions you heard that are used to see both sides of an issue and two expressions that are used to make a compromise.

Seeing both sides of an issue:

1. _____

2. _____

Making a compromise:

1. _____

2. _____

Look back at the statements from "Getting Ready to Listen." Did the simulated radio debate make you think differently about any of your answers?

Science made it possible for the living to donate blood to help others. Now people may face difficult decisions about whether or not to donate the organs of family members who have died in order that others may live in greater health.

PART 2: Staying Human in a Scientific World

Getting Ready to Read

Vocabulary Building

Below are vocabulary words from the newspaper article you are going to read. Each word is used in a sentence. Work with a partner. Try to define the word based on the context.

1. Running a marathon is an amazing athletic **feat.**

   feat (noun) _____

2. The astronauts working on the international space station carefully **coaxed** the wires into the correct position.

   to coax (verb) _____

3. Grey whales, Siberian tigers, and spotted owls are all **endangered** species.

   endangered (adjective) _____

4. After his heart attack he underwent a successful heart **transplant.** His body accepted the new heart.

transplant (noun) _____

5. That can is **misshapen.** I don't think you should eat the soup in that can. You might get food poisoning.

misshapen (adjective) _____

Now match the vocabulary word in Column A with the correct definition in Column B.

COLUMN A	COLUMN B
_____ feat	a. bent, incorrectly shaped
_____ to coax	b. surgery to move something from one body to another
_____ endangered	c. achievement
_____ transplant	d. gently manipulate
_____ misshapen	e. almost eliminated

Read

Mouse Yields Elephant's Egg

1 In a medical feat that sounds like something dreamed up by Dr. Seuss, scientists have coaxed a mouse into growing an elephant egg.

2   The technique could someday be used to help save some of the world's endangered species. Mice could be used as factories to produce eggs of other species; the eggs could then be fertilized and used to impregnate the endangered animals.

3   Purdue University researcher John Critser leads a team that transplanted ovarian tissue from African elephants into lab mice that had been bred so that their bodies would not reject foreign tissue.

4   Several of the mice developed egg-producing follicles, and one contained a mature—though misshapen—egg.

5   The egg was not considered healthy enough to produce a successful pregnancy, but Critser's team had no intention of using it to impregnate an elephant at this point anyway.

> One has to look out for engineers—they begin with sewing machines and end up with atomic bombs.
>
> —MARCEL PAGNOL

After You Read

Discuss your response to the article with a partner. Answer the following questions.

1. Do you think this is a good, bad, or neutral way to use medical technology? Why?

2. How do you feel about the way this research affects the mice? Do you think it is fair to use mice as factories to breed other animals?

3. According to the article, what is one possible positive result of this kind of research? Do you think the result justifies the research and experiments?

LANGUAGE LEARNING STRATEGY

Apply the Strategy

Try to understand whole ideas rather than individual vocabulary words. This will improve your general comprehension more quickly than studying only vocabulary.

In the next activity there are some words that may be new to you. As you do the activity, make sure that you:

1. Don't stop at each new word.

2. Try to understand the general concepts.

3. Don't get stuck—move ahead.

ACADEMIC POWER STRATEGY

Apply the Strategy

Learn to talk about uncomfortable subjects with greater comfort and confidence. In an earlier chapter, you learned that it is important to seek out new ideas and opinions. It is equally important to feel comfortable and confident talking about these new ideas with others. You may disagree with the opinions of other students in your class, or even with your teacher. This is not bad. This is an opportunity for you to learn about other people and why they think or believe the things they do. The experience can give you a bigger, better picture of the concepts and ideas you will study in many of your classes.

Work with a partner. In each of the following situations, you will be asked to decide how you would react to a certain kind of technology or scientific advancement. Think about and discuss the impact of that technology and the reason for your decision. If the topic is uncomfortable:

1. Stop and ask yourself why you feel uncomfortable.

2. Ask yourself why another person might "see" things differently.

(continued on next page)

3. Ask yourself what you can learn from the situation or experience.

4. Then use your language skills to express your ideas and respond to your partner's.

WHAT WOULD YOU DO?

In Part I of this chapter you examined the morality of certain aspects of technology itself. However, in daily life you often make important personal choices about how you use technology or even what technology you will use. You make these choices based on your system of personal values. Perhaps you will not eat fruit that has been sprayed with pesticides even though the pesticides help control the insect population. Perhaps you refuse to use certain convenient household cleaning products because they contain chemicals that damage the environment. In an increasingly technological world, many small choices that you make have much bigger implications about the way you want your world to function now and in the future.

1. You are going blind. Recent medical developments make it possible for the **retina** of a rabbit to be transplanted into the human eye. What would you do?

2. Your spouse is very ill and in a great deal of pain. It is quite certain that your spouse will die within the next two or three months. A doctor in your country has recently invented a machine that makes it possible for people to commit suicide in a quick and painless way. Your spouse would like to use this machine. What would you do?

3. Your country allows selective abortion. You and your spouse are expecting a child. You want a boy child very badly because you already have three daughters. Amniocentesis has shown that this child will also be a girl. It is possible for you to abort this child. What would you do?

4. The cost of electricity in your country is very high. Your government would like to build a nuclear reactor near your town. This would reduce the cost of lighting and heating your home. However, there is a chance that nuclear waste would leak into your water supply. What would you do?

5. You are young and single. Over the next few years you would like to have many positive experiences with members of the opposite sex. It is possible to make use of a semi-permanent form of birth control so that you do not have to think about this all the time; however, this new form of birth control may have serious side effects that have not yet been detected. What would you do?

6. Since the beginning of your marriage you have been trying to start your family, but your wife cannot have a child. Due to recent technological advances you, the husband, have the opportunity to be impregnated and carry the child for nine months. What would you do?

7. You have been in a terrible automobile accident. You have lost all control of your body, but your mind still functions perfectly. Through medical science you can be kept alive indefinitely. What would you do?

8. You and your spouse are planning to have a child. Through recent medical developments it is possible to alter the gene pool and choose specific characteristics for your child. What would you do?

9. Scientists are close to discovering a cure for AIDS. They are currently testing a new medication on animals. The medication limits the disease but produces terrible side effects, such as loss of muscle control. Many animals are suffering as scientists perfect the medication. What would you do?

10. You are a computer expert. Recently you have accidentally discovered how to infiltrate the computerized defense of your country. You know that your country is planning an attack on a hostile and extremely dangerous neighboring nation. The attack would safeguard your country's security but annihilate the other nation. What would you do?

REAL PEOPLE/REAL VOICES

◆ **Getting Ready to Listen**

Modern medical technology has made it possible for doctors to predict some serious medical problems before they occur. Work with a partner. Discuss the following situation:

Cancer runs in your family. Doctors can now give you a test and accurately predict whether or not you carry the gene for cancer and could pass cancer on to your children. Would you take the tests? Would you still want to have children? What if it were your husband or wife? Would you want them to take the tests? Do you think it is a good idea for doctors to give tests to diagnose problems *before* those problems occur?

Listen

Listening 2: Susana's Experiences

As you listen, decide if the following statements are true or false. Circle the correct answer.

1. Susana and her husband were very happy when they learned they were going to have a child.

    True   False

2. The doctor recommended that Susana have some medical tests after the baby was born.

    True   False

3. It is not normal to have prenatal testing.

    True   False

4. Susana's friend refused to take any tests because she didn't want to face difficult choices.

    True   False

5. Doctors can now cure certain illnesses even before the baby is born.

    True   False

6. Susana believes that the tests make it easier to feel good about being pregnant.

    True   False

After You Listen

Look back at the activity "What Would You Do?" on page 178. What would you do in Susana's situation? Would you have the tests? Would you choose not to have the tests? Discuss your answer with a partner. If you and your partner disagree, practice the language of "seeing both sides" in your discussion.

Making a Technological Wish List

1. Go back to the chart of technologies in the values-clarification activity. Come to a consensus with your class about which topic you'd like to debate. The topic you choose should be one of the technologies you rated as "bad" or one that is particularly controversial.

2. The class will divide into two groups: "scientists" and "moralists." The scientists should work in their group to make a "wish list" of five avenues of research they would like to pursue in the chosen

technology. The moralists should make a "wish list" of five limitations they would like to impose on research and development into the chosen technology. These limitations should be decided based on issues of morality.

3. When you have completed your wish list, present your list to the other group. As you state your wishes, the other group will take notes on what you present.

4. After both groups have presented their wishes, return to your individual groups and discuss the wishes that have been presented. Prepare to debate your viewpoint on the wish list of the other group. Use the expressions you have learned in this chapter to demonstrate your understanding of the other side, and be prepared to make compromises.

5. Now you will face the other group and debate the issues. The moralists should begin. State a wish that the scientists have presented and discuss your opposing viewpoint. The scientists can then respond by defending their viewpoint. If possible, come to a compromise. It is then the turn of the scientists to respond to a wish that the moralists presented. Proceed this way until all the wishes have been discussed.

TUNING IN: "Two Sides of Cloning"

© CNN

You will see a CNN video clip about human cloning. Before you watch the clip, talk with a partner and answer these questions.

> What is the first thing that you think of when you think about cloning?
> Do you have a positive response to the idea of cloning or a negative response?
> Do you think of cloning as something that will become more common, or does cloning still seem like science fiction?

As you watch the first time, take notes to summarize the viewpoints of these three people. Listen for the key word in parentheses to help focus on important information.

1. Ian Wilmut (individual) _____

_____

2. Unidentified bioethicist* (regulatory model) _____

_____

*A bioethicist is someone who studies the ethics of science and progress, particularly in areas relating to living creatures.

Man is still the most extraordinary computer of all.

— JOHN F. KENNEDY

3. Art Kaplan (ethical problem) _____

_____

As you watch the second time, decide if each sentence below is true or false according to the video. Circle the correct answer.

1. Nineteen European countries are experimenting with human cloning.

         True   False

2. Ian Wilmut, who helped clone Dolly the sheep, believes that human cloning means cloned children would not be treated as individuals.

         True   False

3. Some bioethicists believe it is possible to regulate human cloning well enough that it would be both safe and ethical.

         True   False

4. It is possible for cloning to be handled like adoption, with a screening process that eliminates parents who might not use the process appropriately.

         True   False

5. Art Kaplan thinks there are no ethical problems related to cloning a child who then looks exactly like one of his or her parents.

         True   False

6. Scientists are ready to clone human beings now.

         True   False

PUTTING IT ALL TOGETHER

1. Think of a situation in the recent past when it was necessary for you to make a compromise. In the future, if you find yourself in a similar situation, what is one way you will be able to express compromise in English?

2. Even if you disagree with someone, can you fairly recognize that person's point of view? How can you use English to express this recognition?

3. List five new science-related words that you have learned in this chapter. Write the definitions beside the words.

   1. _____

   2. _____

3. _____

4. _____

5. _____

4. What is one way that science and morality are in conflict? Is this something you had thought about before? How will it affect future decisions that you make?

Test-Taking Tip

Look for clues from your instructor as to what will be on the examination. Instructors will often repeat important words several times or write them on the board and give handouts. Put yourself in the instructor's head—what questions would you ask? And lastly, be alert for these magic words: "This material will be on the test" or, "This is important—you need to know this."

CHECKING YOUR PROGRESS

On a scale of 1 to 5, rate how well you have mastered the goals set at the beginning of the chapter:

1 2 3 4 5   express both sides of an issue.

1 2 3 4 5   recognize different points of view.

1 2 3 4 5   express compromise.

1 2 3 4 5   analyze the meaning of a new word by relating it to something familiar.

1 2 3 4 5   understand whole ideas rather than individual vocabulary words.

1 2 3 4 5   talk about uncomfortable subjects with greater comfort and confidence.

If you've given yourself a 3 or lower on any of these goals:

- visit the *Tapestry* web site for additional practice.

- ask your instructor for extra help.

- review the sections of the chapter that you found difficult.

- work with a partner or study group to further your progress.

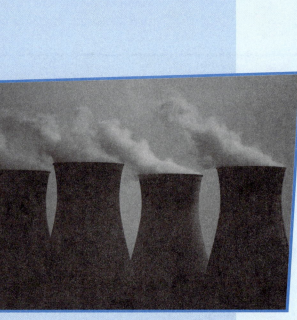

These photographs show the relationship between what we as human beings are capable of producing with the help of technology and the impact that this technology can have on the environment that we live in. Do we have the right to develop without limits using our resources and the technology that we now have? Spend a few minutes discussing this cause/effect relationship.

THE NATURE OF THINGS—ENVIRONMENTAL CONCERNS

In examining our daily lives, it is easy to see the ways that science and technology have made certain tasks easier and more convenient. However, we often worry about setting limits on future development of technology because of concerns about what is ethical. We also worry about how technology affects our environment. There is growing concern around the world about the damage we have done to our planet in our efforts to take technology to its limits. For every gain we have made due to technology, there may be a corresponding loss to the quality of our natural environment. In this chapter, we will be discussing the environment and the concerns that people around the world share for the future of the Earth.

Setting Goals

In this chapter you will learn how to:

◈ identify the purpose of a language task.

◈ express concern and dissatisfaction about specific problems.

◈ state plans and intentions to solve a problem.

◈ develop realistic plans and prioritize them.

◈ identify contrasting viewpoints.

◆Getting Started

Circle True or False for each of the statements below. There are no right or wrong answers. Explain your choices to your partner.

What Do I Think About the Topic?

1. True   False   I am aware of problems concerning the environment.

2. True   False   There is nothing I can do personally to prevent damage to the environment.

3. True   False   It's important for each of us to be concerned about the environment.

4. True   False   There is a lot being done internationally to protect the environment.

5. True   False   It is possible to reverse the damage that has been done to the environment.

6. True   False   Through science and technology, we will find a way to replace the natural resources that are disappearing.

7. True   False   The damage to the environment isn't as bad as some people fear.

8. True   False   It is not too late to take steps to save the environment.

What Do I Know About the Language?

1. In English there are two different meanings for the word *environment*. What do you think the meanings are? Write them on the lines below.

   Meaning 1: _____

   Meaning 2: _____

2. If you are worried or concerned about something, what do you say in English? Write two ways of expressing worry or concern.

   _____

   _____

3. If you are dissatisfied with something, what can you say in English? Write two ways of expressing dissatisfaction.

   _____

   _____

4. If you want to state an intention or a plan, what would you say in English? Write two ways of stating an intention or a plan.

_____

_____

PART 1: Who Cares About the Environment?

Mother Earth—one thing we all share in equally.

Culture Note

The U.S. Environmental Protection Agency (EPA) was established as an independent agency on December 2, 1970. The EPA's mission is to protect human health and to safeguard the natural environment—air, water, and land—upon which life depends. The EPA ensures that federal laws protecting human health and the environment are based on the best available scientific information and are enforced fairly and effectively. The agency is responsible for making information available to the public so that individuals and organizations can make informed decisions about health and environmental risks. Environmental protection contributes to making our communities and ecosystems diverse, sustainable, and economically productive. The EPA works to ensure that environmental protection receives consideration from policy makers and that the United States plays a role in working with other nations to protect the global environment. You can read more about the Environmental Protection Agency online at: http://www.epa.gov/.

LANGUAGE LEARNING STRATEGY

Identify the purpose of a language task. When you are studying English, you are often asked to complete language tasks. These are activities and exercises which ask you to use the language you are learning for a specific purpose. If you can identify the purpose of a task, you will see how the task can help your language improvement. You will then feel more motivated to complete the task. As a result, you will benefit more from the task. In order to identify the purpose of a language task, follow these steps:

1. Define what the task requires of you. How can you complete the task?

2. Complete the task. Use the language you are learning to do the exercise or activity.

3. Determine the benefits of the task. How did the task help you to learn the language?

4. Summarize the purpose of the task.

Apply the Strategy

"Brainstorming" is a language task in which you work with a group to generate ideas quickly and freely. During a brainstorming activity you don't evaluate or monitor the ideas you have. All ideas are acceptable. Next, you will complete a brainstorming task. As you complete the task, follow the steps to identify the purpose of the task.

> To cherish what remains of the earth and to foster its renewal is our only legitimate hope of survival.
>
> **—WENDELL BERRY**

Step 1: Define What the Task Requires of You

Read the directions for the brainstorming task under Step 2 below. After you read the directions, define what the task requires of you by completing the statement which follows the directions.

Step 2: Complete the Task

Divide into small groups. With your group, make a list of all the environmental problems that concern you. Write your list on the lines provided. Use brainstorming to help each other complete the list. Write your list as you do the brainstorming.

In order to complete the brainstorming task, I must _____

_____

_____

_____

BRAINSTORMING: ENVIRONMENTAL PROBLEMS

1. _____   6. _____

2. _____   7. _____

3. _____   8. _____

4. _____   9. _____

5. _____   10. _____

Step 3: Determine the Benefits of the Task

As you complete the brainstorming task, check the benefits below that you agree with.

_____ You can think quickly because all of your ideas are acceptable.

_____ Hearing the ideas of others stimulates more ideas from you.

_____ Hearing the ideas of others helps you to focus on the topic.

_____ You have less fear about your ideas because everyone is sharing their ideas.

Step 4: Summarize the Purpose of the Task

Complete the statement below to summarize the purpose of the brainstorming task.

I think the purpose of the brainstorming task is to _____

_____

Write About It.

Think about the environmental concerns that you listed in the brainstorming activity. Which are the ones that concern you most? What can you do about these concerns? Write your ideas below.

_____

_____

_____

_____

_____

_____

LANGUAGE YOU CAN USE: EXPRESSING CONCERN/EXPRESSING DISSATISFACTION

The chart below contains expressions that are used to express concern or to express dissatisfaction—for example, about environmental problems. There are also expressions that can be used to discuss your plans for solving these problems.

EXPRESSING CONCERN	EXAMPLES
What worries me is that . . .	*What worries me is that* the weather has become so extreme.
What concerns me is . . .	*What concerns me is* the drought.
Something that concerns/worries me is . . .	*Something that worries me is* how much paper we waste. (This expression is followed by a noun, noun phrase, or noun clause.)

EXPRESSING DISSATISFACTION	
What I really can't stand is when . . .	*What I really can't stand is when* people blame environmental problems on immigrants.
What I really hate is when . . .	*What I really hate is when* technology is seen as the cause of environmental problems.
What really bothers me is when . . .	*What really bothers me is when* my dictionary doesn't include a word I need.

STATING PLANS/INTENTIONS	
What I'd like to do is . . .	*What I'd like to do is* buy a better English dictionary.
What I plan is to . . .	*What I plan is to* form a committee on campus to recycle paper.
What I intend to do is . . .	*What I intend to do is* volunteer for the project to clean up the bay.

USING NEW LANGUAGE

History was made in upstate New York on October 15, 1998 when the first green-certified paper in North America was produced. It was certified because it came from soundly managed forests.

With a partner, use the language in the chart to discuss concern or dissatisfaction you currently feel about learning English. Then discuss the goals you have that would address these concerns.

EXAMPLE: Concern: I'm really worried because I don't feel like I'm making any progress.

Plan: What I plan is to get a tutor so that I can make faster progress.

1. Concern: _____

    Plan: _____

2. Concern: _____

    Plan: _____

Now, with a partner, use the language in the chart to express any concern or dissatisfaction you feel about the environment. Then discuss the plans you can make to address these concerns.

EXAMPLE: Concern: Something that concerns me is that I don't know about environmental problems.

Plan: What I intend to do is choose this topic for my research paper so that I can learn more.

1. Concern: _____

     Plan: _____

2. Concern: _____

     Plan: _____

ACADEMIC POWER STRATEGY

Develop realistic plans and prioritize them. When striving for academic success, it is very helpful to develop realistic plans. These plans will give you direction and increase your energy and determination to succeed. Once you have a set of plans, you must determine whether they are realistic. If your plans are unrealistic, you will get frustrated because you will feel the impossibility of achieving them. Finally, when you have a set of realistic plans, you should prioritize them. By deciding which plans are most important, you can avoid feeling overwhelmed and move forward more efficiently. Follow these steps:

1. Develop a set of plans.

2. Determine whether the plans are realistic.

3. Prioritize the plans.

Apply the Strategy

In a discussion of environment, we should also include discussion of our academic environment. Our academic environment includes whatever our physical surroundings are when we study. For example, academic environment includes our personal work space, our desk, the classroom, the school, the campus, the library, and the bookstore. Think about the conditions in your academic environment that you would like to change in order to improve your study time or your ability to succeed in your studies. Then follow the steps below.

> **The trouble with our times is that the future is not what it used to be.**
>
> **—PAUL VALERY**

Step 1: With a partner, make a list of plans for improving your academic environment. List anything that would help you to do better at your studies. The plans can be things that you would do yourself or things that others could do. (Examples: "What I intend to do is clean up my desk." "What we plan is to get the library to make one area a 'no talking zone.' ")

_____   _____

_____   _____

_____   _____

_____   _____

Step 2: Look at your list of plans in Step 1. Determine whether each plan is realistic. Cross out any plans that are not realistic.

Step 3: Prioritize the list of realistic plans you now have by writing the most important plan first, the next-most-important one second, etc.

1. _____

2. _____

3. _____

4. _____

5. _____

PART 2: Taking Action

◆ **Getting Ready to Read**

Recycling is a plan that helps with environmental protection. You are going to read about such a recycling effort that arose in the manufacturing and retail industries. Discuss the following questions before reading the passage:

1. Do you think that we live in a wasteful society?

2. Why is it important to recycle?

3. Why is recycling more important today than it was 100 years ago?

4. If you had an old TV that didn't work anymore, what would you do with it?

◆ **Read**

Guessing Meaning from Context

As you read the passage, discuss with a partner the meaning of each vocabulary item listed on the following page. Tell your partner what you think the word means by guessing from the context of the reading. Then find out from your teacher or a dictionary how accurate your guesses are.

1. **efficiency**

    Student 1: _____

    Student 2: _____

2. **compost**

    Student 1: _____

    Student 2: _____

3. **durables**

    Student 1: _____

    Student 2: _____

4. **components**

    Student 1: _____

    Student 2: _____

5. **indefinitely**

    Student 1: _____

    Student 2: _____

Magic Carpet

1 The key to resource **efficiency** is to understand products as a means to deliver a service to the customer, rather than thinking of them as *things*. . . . Braungart and McDonough advanced a new way to conceive of products, breaking them down into three categories: consumables, products of service and unmarketables.

2   . . . Consumables are products like bananas, jute or aspirin that can harmlessly go back to the soil as **compost.** Products of service are usually **durables** such as cars, TVs, and refrigerators. Braungart and McDonough argue that these products should be "licensed" in the same way that software is today. The product would always belong to the manufacturer, but unlike software, it would eventually get returned to the manufacturer, who would be responsible for recycling or reusing the product. Manufacturers would have to design and create their products so that all **components** have value when they return (just as in nature), and not just when they leave the factory. . . .

3   . . . With a "products as service" system, customers could keep a product **indefinitely** or sell it to others, just as they do now. The final user, when finished, would take it to a de-shopping center that would return it to the manufacturer for reuse and remanufacturing.

◆After You Read

Read the article a second time; then discuss these questions with your classmates:

1. What is the goal of a "products as service" system?

2. Do you think this kind of system could be successful?

3. What concerns might you have about its effectiveness?

LANGUAGE LEARNING STRATEGY

Identify the contrasting viewpoints when you listen to a debate. This will increase your understanding of the debate. As you listen, try to determine what the arguments are and why the speakers agree or disagree. State the issue being discussed and listen for the main point each speaker makes about the issue. After the debate, summarize how the view of one speaker contrasts with the view of another speaker.

For example, you can apply this strategy to the following exchange:

Speaker A: I don't recycle because I don't think it really helps to improve the environment.

Speaker B: Of course it makes a difference. If all of us don't recycle, we will soon run out of space to dump all the garbage we produce.

1. Issue being discussed: Recycling

2. Main points: Speaker A doesn't recycle and doesn't think that it affects the environment. Speaker B thinks that recycling lessens the amount of garbage that is dumped.

3. Summary of contrasting views: Speaker A thinks that recycling is useless while Speaker B thinks that recycling can help save the environment.

(continued on next page)

Apply the Strategy

You are going to hear a discussion between two people. Robert Stevens, who is a guest speaker on a talk radio show, is an environmentalist. Frank Grant calls in to discuss the impact of technology on the environment. As you do the exercises below, apply the strategy of identifying contrasting viewpoints.

 Getting Ready to Listen

Before you listen to the discussion, think about these questions. What are some arguments against the development of technology based on the damage it has done to the environment? What are some arguments supporting the development of technology to help improve the environment? Make a list of the contrasting viewpoints on the lines below.

Against Development of Technology:

_____

_____

_____

_____

Air pollution may be responsible for 5% of hospital admissions for heart disease.

For Development of Technology:

_____

_____

_____

_____

Listen

Listening 1: Discussing the Environment

As you listen, identify the contrasting viewpoints by completing the exercise below.

1. Issue Being Discussed

   On the lines below, state the issue being discussed:

   _____

   _____

2. Main Points of Each Speaker

   Listen for the main points that each speaker makes about the issue being discussed. Write the main points below the correct name.

Stevens	Grant
_____	_____
_____	_____
_____	_____

After You Listen

Write a summary of the contrasting views of the speakers.

Stevens thinks that _____

_____

while Grant thinks that _____

_____

The Sound of It: Understanding Reductions

On the tape, the speakers used several reductions. Listen to the tape again. Listen to the reduced form for each sentence below. Then write the original form for that sentence.

> Technological progress has merely provided us with more efficient means for going backwards.
>
> —ALDOUS HUXLEY

1. Reduced Form: One a the biggest problems we're facing . . .

   Original Form: _____

2. Reduced Form: Doncha see the impact this technological advance has had?

   Original Form: _____

3. Reduced Form: I understandjer point, Mr. Grant . . .

   Original Form: _____

4. Reduced Form: Of course I see that, but lookit th'development technology has made.

   Original Form: _____

5. Reduced Form: . . . t'cut down on th'pollution caused by so many people driving to work . . .

   Original Form: _____

TUNING IN: "An Ecovillage"

You are going to watch a video about an "ecovillage." This is a village in which the design and lifestyle decrease the amount of harm to the environment. What do you think some of the characteristics

© CNN

of the village might be? Work with a partner and use your brainstorming skills to list some possible characteristics.

EXAMPLE: solar heating

1. _____

2. _____

3. _____

4. _____

5. _____

As you watch the video and complete the two listening tasks below, try to determine the purpose of the activities.

Viewing Task 1

Watch the video and place a check next to the features that describe Ecovillage.

_____ solar heating   _____ community banking

_____ no paved roads   _____ organic gardening

_____ carpooling   _____ shared energy

_____ recycled garbage   _____ vegetarian menu

Viewing Task 2

Watch the video again and listen for reasons why the residents of Ecovillage decided to become part of the community. Write the reasons on the lines below.

_____

_____

_____

_____

_____

Discussion

With a partner, discuss whether you'd like to live in Ecovillage. After your discussion, write one reason why your partner would like to live there and one reason why your partner would not like to live there.

My partner would like to live there because

_____

_____

_____

My partner would not like to live there because

_____

_____

_____

In recent years, there has been an increased awareness of the importance of recycling. The three Rs to keep in mind for a cleaner environment are: reduce, reuse, and recycle. Reducing is the best way to protect the environment. However, if you can't reduce something, reuse it, and if you can't reuse it, recycle it. Reducing waste means shopping with the environment in mind. Consider the environmental impact of each product before you buy it. Make a list of what you need before you go shopping; this will reduce impulse buying. Buy in bulk—it's cheaper and eliminates small containers and excess packaging. Avoid buying things that can't be recycled.

Learning to reuse is easy after a little practice. For example, you can reuse shopping bags or buy canvas bags and use them when you shop. Buy durable, high-quality goods for a longer life outside the landfill. Although durable goods may cost a little more at first, they will save you money and help save the environment in the long run. Before throwing anything away, think about how each item can be reused.

Recycling means collecting, processing, marketing, and ultimately reusing materials that were once discarded. Check the yellow pages or the Internet to find information about local recycling programs in your community.

PROBLEM-SOLVING ACTIVITY: EARTH DAY CONFERENCE

Situation: You and your classmates have been elected to represent your school and your city at a conference on environmental protection being held on Earth Day. Work with a small group of your classmates to complete the following tasks.

Task 1: Look at the brainstorming activity you completed at the beginning of the chapter. Choose one concern that you would like to focus on at the conference. Use the language you studied in this chapter to write your concern on the lines.

_____

_____

_____

Task 2: Use the language you have learned in this chapter to discuss and list the specific concerns or dissatisfaction you feel about this issue.

1. _____
2. _____
3. _____
4. _____
5. _____

Task 3: Discuss and list the steps you think should be taken so that changes can be made concerning this issue.

1. _____
2. _____
3. _____
4. _____
5. _____

REAL PEOPLE/REAL VOICES

On the tape you will hear two students speaking about their experiences. Chen is a student at a community college in the United States. Rafael is a student in an intensive English program at a university in the United States.

◀Getting Ready to Listen

You will listen to Chen and Rafael having a conversation about their study environment. They have contrasting viewpoints about what makes a good study environment. Before you listen, work with a partner to list three things that make a good study environment and three things that make a bad study environment.

Good Study Environment

1. _____

2. _____

3. _____

Bad Study Environment

1. _____

2. _____

3. _____

◀Listen

Listening 2: Chen's and Rafael's Experiences

As you listen, write **C** next to the statement below if it is true about Chen and **R** next to the statement if it is true about Rafael.

1. _____ I get average grades.

2. _____ I don't study well in the library.

3. _____ I study very well at my desk.

4. _____ When there are people around, it gives me the energy to study.

5. _____ If I listen to music while I study, I get distracted.

6. _____ I do well on tests.

7. _____ The noisier it is, the better I study.

PUTTING IT ALL TOGETHER

Take turns with your classmates to complete the following tasks. Write your answers on the lines provided. This activity will help list and measure the things you learned in this chapter.

1. List two environmental issues that you learned about in this chapter.

   _____

   _____

   _____

   _____

2. Begin each statement below with expressions used to state goals.

   a. _____ organize a work party to clean up the graffiti at our school.

   b. _____ start a campaign to improve public transportation.

   c. _____ carpool to school at least once a week.

3. List two goals you have for improving your academic environment.

   _____

   _____

   _____

   _____

4. Summarize the opposing viewpoints of the following conversation in your own words:

   Speaker A: We have to limit immigration because our resources cannot handle the masses of people coming to this country.

   Speaker B: Rather than seeing immigration as the problem, we should find more efficient ways to live so that we can avoid draining our natural resources.

   Speaker A thinks that _____

   _____

   while Speaker B thinks that _____

   _____

Test-Taking Tip

Make sure you are physically rested and ready for exams. The night before an exam, be sure to get a good night's sleep. It is hard to concentrate and do your best when you are exhausted. It is also important to eat at least a light breakfast. You cannot function well on an empty stomach.

CHECK YOUR PROGRESS

On a scale of 1 to 5, rate how well you have mastered the goals set at the beginning of this chapter:

1 2 3 4 5   identify the purpose of a language task.

1 2 3 4 5   express concern and dissatisfaction about specific problems.

1 2 3 4 5   state plans and intentions to solve a problem.

1 2 3 4 5   develop realistic plans and prioritize them.

1 2 3 4 5   identify contrasting viewpoints.

If you've given yourself a 3 or lower on any of these goals:

- visit the *Tapestry* web site for additional practice.
- ask your instructor for extra help.
- review the sections of the chapter that you found difficult.
- work with a partner or study group to further your progress.

T his photograph shows a crowded subway in Tokyo, Japan, where the pace of life is fast and people live under a lot of stress. Could you find a similar scene where you live? What other kinds of situations cause people to feel stress? Discuss these questions with your class.

10

ALL STRESSED OUT
AND NO PLACE TO GO

Throughout this book, we have discussed many issues that influence modern life. We have examined politics, economic difficulties, environmental dangers, family crises, and many other topics that are not always pleasant or easy to talk about. In daily life, these same issues often cause a great deal of stress and worry as people make an effort to live happily and healthily in a rapidly changing world. In this last chapter, we will be examining the stress of modern life—stress resulting from financial worries, political turmoil, changing family structures, relationships, and other common worries. You will review the language you studied in earlier chapters so that you can strengthen your ability to use that language in realistic situations.

Setting Goals

In this chapter you will review:

◈ expressing concern.

◈ asking for clarification.

◈ expressing empathy.

◈ making a suggestion.

205

◆**Getting Started**

How Do I Feel About the Topic?

Complete the following statements to examine some of your feelings about the topic of this chapter.

1. One thing that really makes me feel stress is _____.

2. When I feel stressed, I _____.

3. One change I would like to make in my life is _____.

4. I feel _____ when I have to make a change in my life.

What Do I Know About the Language?

1. If I want to express concern about my grades, I can say: _____
   _____

2. An expression I use to ask for clarification is: _____
   _____

3. When I want to express empathy, I can say: _____
   _____

4. If I wanted to make a suggestion to a friend about meeting assignment deadlines, I would say: _____
   _____

PART 1: What's Stressing You?

RANKING ACTIVITY: HOW STRESSFUL IS IT?

Stress = A feeling of overpowering pressure that comes from situations in one's life.

Look at the list below. All the situations listed can cause stress. Individually, rank each item. Use the scale from 1 to 4 to show how stressful you personally find the situation. Then discuss your list with a partner.

1 = not stressful	3 = somewhat stressful
2 = a little stressful	4 = very stressful

1. _____ getting caught in traffic or missing the bus

2. _____ money problems, the state of the economy

3. _____ overcrowding/noise

4. _____ crime

5. _____ academic pressures: grades, assignments, deadlines

6. _____ environmental dangers

7. _____ break-up of relationships (divorce, separation, etc.)

8. _____ political situations (war, boundary disputes, etc.)

9. _____ lack of privacy

10. _____ pressures of balancing work and family

With a small group of your classmates, look at your list. Answer the following questions:

1. Which item on the list do you find most stressful? Why?

   _____

2. Which item on the list do you find least stressful? Why?

   _____

You may experience all the above situations when you're in your native culture as well as when you're in an English-speaking culture. However, some of these situations may be more stressful when you're in your native culture. Others may be more stressful when you're in an English-speaking culture. This is because there are different kinds of stress that we feel when we are in a foreign culture speaking a language different from our native language. Which situations are most stressful when you're outside of your culture?

LANGUAGE YOU CAN USE:
CONCERN, CLARIFICATION, EMPATHY, AND SUGGESTIONS

Review the following expressions which were covered in previous chapters in this book. Then practice using them in the exercise that follows.

EXPRESSING CONCERN

I'm really worried/concerned because . . .

I'm concerned/worried about . . .

Something that concerns/worries me is . . .

ASKING FOR CLARIFICATION

So, what you really mean is . . .

What exactly are you getting at?

GIVING CLARIFICATION

What I'm trying to say is . . .

What I mean is . . .

MAKING A SUGGESTION

Have you thought about . . . ?

Why don't you . . . ?

Maybe you could . . .

You should/ought to . . .

EXPRESSING EMPATHY

I understand how you can feel that way . . .

I'm sorry that you . . .

USING NEW LANGUAGE

Go back to the ranking activity, and in pairs respond to each of the situations using the expressions in the table preceding this activity. Look at the example below before you begin.

Student A (*expressing concern*): I'm really worried about the final exam.

Student B (*asking for clarification*): What exactly are you getting at?

Student A (*giving clarification*): What I mean is I don't think I've understood a lot of the material, and I don't feel prepared.

Student B (*expressing empathy*): I understand how you can feel that way. We've covered some very difficult concepts. (*making a suggestion*) Have you thought about getting some help from the professor during her office hours?

Write About It.

How do you act when you're feeling stressed? What do you do to relax when you feel stressed?

_____

_____

_____

_____

_____

_____

TUNING IN: "Student Stress"

© CNN

You are going to watch a video comparing students in the United States with students in Japan and China. The video focuses on the stress level of these students. Before you watch the video, answer the questions below:

1. How stressed do you get when you are a student in school?

2. What do you do to relieve your stress when you are studying?

3. Do you think that students from Japan and China or students from the United States would feel more stress in school?

As you watch the video, listen to the following statements. If the statement is about a student from the United States, write **US.** If the statement is about a student from Japan or China, write **JC.**

1. _____ I get really frustrated with school.

2. _____ School is fun, so I don't have any reason to be stressed about it.

3. _____ There's no pressure here for us to study.

4. _____ We get stressed at least once a day.

5. _____ School is central to our life.

6. _____ We have multiple goals.

7. _____ I work 30–35 hours a week, and I play sports.

8. _____ If we get bad grades, we can't advance in class level, so that's what puts the pressure on us.

What questions do you have about the stress level of students from the United States, Japan, and China? After you watch the video, work with a partner to write two questions you have about this.

1. _____

2. _____

The Sound of It: Prepositions with Two-Word Verbs

Sometimes, it is difficult to hear the separate words when you hear a two-word verb. There are several two-word verbs used in the video about student stress. Listen to the two-word verbs and write the preposition that is used after the verb.

1. blow   _____
2. bogged _____
3. gnaws   _____
4. chew   _____
5. spit   _____

LANGUAGE LEARNING STRATEGY

After you listen to something you need to remember, write a summary of it. Then check it for logic and accuracy. When you hear something, you will remember more of it if you write a summary of what you've heard. After you write the summary, you can check it to be sure that you have represented the logic of the original. You can also check to be sure that you have presented the information accurately.

Apply the Strategy

Listen to the following excerpt from a call-in talk radio show on the topic of stress management. The speaker is going to discuss the signals of high stress and methods of stress management. Listen and take notes on the following page. Then, on a separate sheet of paper write a short summary of what you heard. Exchange your summary with a partner to check for logic and accuracy. Then listen to the tape one more time to make additional changes.

LISTEN FOR THE LANGUAGE: TECHNIQUES FOR MANAGING STRESS

Brain cells "talk to each other" by means of chemical messengers. When a person is exposed to too much stress, chemical communication in the brain begins to fail, a condition which is called overstress.

Signals of High Stress

_____

_____

_____

_____

Methods of Stress Management

_____

_____

_____

_____

ACADEMIC POWER STRATEGY

Manage the stress of academic deadlines, tests, and schedules. When you can manage the stress of academic deadlines, tests, and schedules, you will do better in school. Very often you can become anxious or worried that you will not be able to complete assignments, pass tests, or meet deadlines for your classes. However, if you can manage these stressful feelings, you will not become overwhelmed by them. In order to manage this kind of stress, follow these steps:

1. Pay attention to the signals that you are feeling stress.

2. Use specific methods to manage the stress.

Apply the Strategy

Look at your notes from the tape you heard about techniques for managing stress. Think about a time either in the present or the past when you have felt stress about your academic work. What are two signals that you were feeling stress? Write them on the lines on the next page. Then share these with a partner. Ask your partner to suggest specific methods that you could have used to manage the stress. Write down your partner's suggestions.

(continued on next page)

Signals of Your Academic Stress

1 _____

2. _____

Methods for Managing Your Academic Stress

1 _____

2. _____

◈ Getting Ready to Read

Discuss the following questions with a partner before you read the passage about worry.

1. What kinds of things make you worry?

2. What are you worried about right now?

3. Why do some people worry more than others?

4. What situation in your life made you the most worried?

5. What is the best way to treat worry?

> **The better work men do is always done under stress and at great personal cost.**
>
> **—WILLIAM CARLOS WILLIAMS**

Read

Worry

1 Worry is like blood pressure: you need a certain level to live, but too much can kill you. . . . People who worry too much suffer. For all their hard work, for all their humor and willingness to laugh at themselves, for all their self-awareness, worriers just cannot achieve peace of mind.

2 Worry is amazingly common. At least one in four of us—about 65 million Americans—will meet the criteria for an anxiety disorder at some point in our lifetime. Even those individuals whose lives are going well may worry excessively on occasion.

3 And yet, worry is a very treatable condition. Most people today are not aware of all that we have learned about worry in the last 50 years. Just as rainstorms may strike in different ways—sudden thunderstorms, lingering drizzle, occasional showers—so does worry attack its victims variously. We've come to understand the many distinctly different types of worry, and the underlying triggers. Worry may accompany simple shyness, depression, generalized anxiety disorder, or even post-traumatic stress disorder. Each kind of worry responds to specific and powerful techniques, from cognitive therapy to medication to regular exercise.

After You Read

Vocabulary Building

Below are words taken from the reading. There are three synonyms following each word. Use the skills you've developed in the preceding chapters to guess the correct meaning from the context. For each word, circle the choice that best matches the meaning in the reading.

1. **criteria**

   a. rules   b. norms   c. standards

2. **disorder**

   a. problem   b. mess   c. confusion

3. **lingering**

   a. continuing   b. waiting   c. standing

4. **trigger**

   a. encouragement   b. prevention   c. stimulation

5. **traumatic**

   a. alarming   b. sad   c. nervous

PART 2: Self-Development and Change

In this part of the chapter, you will think about methods for dealing with problems and stressful situations. You will also discuss the way that life changes can have an influence on self-development.

Generally speaking, North Americans discuss their feelings and details of their personal lives more openly than do people of some other cultures. This may seem aggressive or impolite if you come from a culture where there is a higher regard for privacy. In North American culture, however, discussion of your personal life is a way of getting closer to someone. For example, you could sit next to someone on a bus or an airplane and by the end of the ride know many personal details about the person's life.

Discussion

With whom would you discuss each of the following issues? Under what circumstances would the issue be too personal to discuss?

a. your level of self-esteem

b. your marriage or divorce

c. painful childhood experiences

d. your romantic experiences

e. an addiction that you have

f. academic failure

LANGUAGE LEARNING STRATEGY

Use a chart to list problems and solutions. This helps you break down one general problem into more specific problems and solutions. When you do this, you can identify each problem clearly and discuss solutions that fit each particular problem. Follow these steps when using a chart to list problems and solutions:

1. Before you use the chart, make a statement that identifies the general problem.

2. Use a chart format to organize the problems and solutions into two lists.

3. Write a heading for each list at the top of the chart. Write Problems on the left-hand side and Solutions on the right-hand side.

4. Break down the larger problem into smaller problems and list them on the left-hand side under Problems.

5. Under Solutions, write the solution for each of the smaller problems.

Apply the Strategy   Follow the steps you learned above and use a chart to list problems and solutions in the next exercise.

PROBLEM SOLVING

Another way to minimize stress and make improvements in your life is to make small but definite changes in your own behavior or lifestyle to solve problems. In this exercise, you are going to read about several different problems. The solutions to these problems are related to personal development. After the description of the problems, you will find a list of methods used for problem solving and personal development. Read the description of each problem. Discuss with the members of your group why it is a problem, and make one statement identifying the general problem. Then, in the chart provided, make a list of the various problems that result from the initial situation. Decide what you would recommend for solutions to each of the related problems, and write that in the chart. For the solutions to the problems, you may choose from the list provided or add others of your own. The first one is done for you.

Problem 1: Judy is a single mother with two kids. She has a full-time job and a part-time job in order to support her kids. Her jobs are very demanding, and she is always tired. She feels stressed out and guilty that she doesn't have more time for her kids.

Statement of problem: _Judy is working too much and doesn't feel like she spends enough time with her kids._

Problem 2: Larry is an alcoholic college student. When he wakes up in the morning, he mixes liquor in his coffee. During breaks between classes, he drinks a few beers. Most nights of the week, he goes out and gets drunk.

Statement of problem: _____

_____

Problem 3: Ruth had a very close friend who recently died of AIDS. She is filled with grief and is finding it difficult to carry on with her life.

Statement of problem: _____

_____

Problem 4: Kevin has low self-esteem. He doesn't have much confidence in himself and doesn't believe he can achieve professional success or get along socially. For example, when an opportunity comes up for a better job that he is qualified for, he won't apply because he thinks that he won't be able to do the job as well as someone else. He avoids social situations because he thinks that people won't accept him.

Statement of problem: _____

_____

Problem 5: Steve has a problem with obesity. He is 50 pounds overweight. He has tried a number of diets, but nothing has worked.

Statement of problem: _____

_____

Problem 6: Carol and Richard are having marital problems. They have been married for nine years and recently have not been getting along well at all. They have a two-year-old daughter. They are thinking about a legal separation.

Statement of problem: _____

_____

Methods of Self-Development

Reading books	Work	Shopping
Talking to a friend	Rehabilitation	Religion
Thinking	Hospitalization	Change of residence
Travel	Psychotherapy	Money
Support group	Drugs	Meditation
Astrology	Exercise	

Problems	Solutions
1. She is always tired. She's doing too much. If she's stressed out, it will affect her kids. She feels guilty. She feels alone.	Schedule time for herself. Try to find one job that pays more. Get help with the housework. Therapy Support group
2.	
3.	
4.	
5.	
6.	

The attitude towards change is different from one culture to another. In North America, change is looked upon positively and is often considered a sign of personal development. For example, in the United States it is not uncommon for people to move a number of times from one house or apartment to another. This attitude towards change is connected to the history of this country. People from other cultures have come to America to start a new life and change something about the life they were living. This attitude toward change may be different from the culture in which you were raised.

Making a Change

One way that you develop as an individual is by making certain changes in yourself and in your life. Some changes are made because you make a decision to make a change. Others are out of your control. Discuss the life changes below and answer these questions about each one:

1. Have you ever made this kind of change in your life?

2. Were you responsible for the change, or was it out of your control?

3. How did the change make you feel? What were the benefits and drawbacks?

4. What adjustments had to be made when this change occurred?

    Life Changes

    a. move from one city to another

    b. move from one country to another

    c. cut your hair/shave a beard off

    d. weight loss/weight gain

    e. change of religion

    f. marriage

    g. divorce

    h. childbirth

    i. death of a loved one

    j. change of job

    k. graduation from a university

    l. learning a new language

REAL PEOPLE/REAL VOICES

 Getting Ready to Listen

> The world is so fast that there are days when the person who says it can't be done is interrupted by the person who is doing it.
>
> —ANONYMOUS

You are going to hear two people talking about the stress in their lives. Andrew is a student who has just finished his first semester at college. Henry is a working man with children. For each of them, make one prediction about what causes them stress. Write down your prediction on the line.

Andrew—college student

I think _____ causes Andrew stress.

Henry—working parent

I think _____ causes Henry stress.

Listen

Listening 1: Andrew's and Henry's Experiences

Write **A** if the statement is true about Andrew and **H** if the statement is true about Henry.

1. _____ Worries give him the most stress.

2. _____ He has a frantic schedule.

3. _____ Academic pressure makes him nervous.

4. _____ He worries about his kids.

5. _____ Sport helps him to deal with stress.

6. _____ Solving one problem at a time helps him to deal with stress.

After You Listen

For each of the two speakers you heard on the tape, give a suggestion for how he can deal with his stress.

Andrew: _____

Henry: _____

The Sound of It: "Filler" Sounds and Words

In spoken language, a *filler* is a sound or word that fills in the space and gives the speaker time to think before continuing. In spoken English, "um" is the most common filler. It's important to recognize this sound so that you don't confuse it with part of another word. Listen to the tape again, and count the number of times each speaker uses the filler "um."

Andrew: _____

Henry: _____

PUTTING IT ALL TOGETHER

1. List two methods you can use to manage the academic stress of deadlines, tests, and schedules.

   a. _____

   b. _____

2. Use the language you have reviewed in this chapter to ask for clarification, give clarification, express empathy, and make a suggestion in the following situation.

   A: I'm so stressed out. I never feel relaxed.

   B (*ask for clarification*): _____

   _____

   A (*give clarification*): _____

   _____

   B (*express empathy*): _____

   _____

   B (*give a suggestion*): _____

   _____

3. List two signals of stress that you learned about in this chapter:

   a. _____

   b. _____

Test-Taking Tip

The night before the test, set aside all the things you need to have with you at the test, including pens, pencils, erasers, a watch, etc. You may also need tissues, cough drops, etc. Coming to the test with everything you need will ensure that you won't be distracted by these details during the test.

CHECK YOUR PROGRESS

On a scale of 1 to 5, rate how well you have mastered the goals set at the beginning of this chapter:

1 2 3 4 5   expressing concern.

1 2 3 4 5   asking for clarification.

1 2 3 4 5   expressing empathy.

1 2 3 4 5   making a suggestion.

If you've given yourself a 3 or lower on any of these goals:

- visit the *Tapestry* web site for additional practice.
- ask your instructor for extra help.
- review the sections of the chapter that you found difficult.
- work with a partner or study group to further your progress.

APPENDIX
SIMULATIONS FOR CHAPTER 2, PAGES 43–44

Simulation 1

Partner A: You are talking with a classmate about your future plans in the United States or another English-speaking country. In your culture, it is very important to maintain eye contact, to look in another person's eyes when you talk to him or her. This shows that you are honest and friendly. Try to look directly in your classmate's eyes as you talk. If your partner looks away, reestablish eye contact.

Partner B: You are talking with a classmate about your future plans in the United States or another English-speaking country. In your culture it is very rude to look directly in someone's eyes. Do not look your partner in the eyes. Look away. If your classmate looks directly in your eyes, turn your face to avoid this rude, aggressive eye contact.

Simulation 2

Partner A: You have met your friend at the grocery store. You want to stop and invite your friend to a party at your home. In your culture, it is very polite to stand very close to your friends. This shows warmth and liking for the other person. When people move away from you, you naturally move closer to them. Stay very close to your partner.

Partner B: You have met your friend at the grocery store. Your friend wants to talk and invite you to a party at his home. In your culture, it is rude to stand close to another person. You want to be several feet away from other people at all times. When a person moves close to you, you naturally move away. Don't stand close to your partner.

Simulation 3

Partner A: You have met a new student at school. You would like to become friends with this student.

In your culture, people show their desire to get to know someone by asking that person a lot of questions. Ask your new classmate as many questions as you can.

Partner B: You have met a new student at school. This person seems to want to get to know you. He asks you a lot of questions. You feel uncomfortable. In your culture, it is very rude to talk about yourself or to ask personal questions. You don't want to answer any questions, and you will not ask any questions.

Simulation 4

Partner A: You and a friend are choosing a movie to see this evening. You have the newspaper. In your culture, the speed of conversation is very fast. People do not wait to answer questions. They answer immediately. If a person does not answer a question right away, you assume he did not hear and repeat the question or ask another question.

Partner B: You and a friend are choosing a movie to see this evening. You have the newspaper. In your culture, the speed of conversation is slow. When someone asks you questions, you pause before answering to show that you have listened carefully and are thinking before you answer. Wait at least eight seconds before answering any question. Look around the room. If someone asks you a lot of questions very quickly, you become confused and you do not understand what he wants.

Simulation 5

Partner A: You are a teacher. One student in your class has worked very hard and made a lot of progress. You want to praise the student. In your culture, praise and compliments are ways to encourage someone to keep improving. They build confidence.

You want the student to feel good and have more self-esteem. Give the student a lot of compliments.

Partner B: You are a student from another country. In your culture it is very rude to accept compliments or praise. When a person gives you a compliment, you must disagree and tell that person that she is mistaken. You do this to show that you are not proud, but modest and humble. You must point out all your faults and mistakes. Never agree with a person who gives you a compliment.

Simulation 6

Partner A: You are a student. You are going to see a teacher because you missed his class when you were sick. You want to get the information you missed. In your culture, time is very valuable. You must get right down to business. It is rude to waste a moment of someone else's time. You do not want to waste the teacher's time by making a lot of small talk.

Partner B: You are a teacher. One of your students has come to your office. He missed a class. He wants the information he missed. It is important to show the student that you are interested in him before discussing business matters. You want to be caring and concerned about the student. You ask a lot of questions about his health, other classes, job away from school, etc. You put off giving the student the information and make small talk first to be friendly.

SCENARIO ACTIVITIES FOR CHAPTER 3, PAGES 55–57

Scenario Activities: Descriptions of Female Roles

1. You and your husband live in a very nice two-bedroom apartment. You have been thinking recently about how pleasant it would be to buy a house someday. You cannot afford a new house now. You're just curious about the kind of house your husband would like to live in when you can afford it.
2. You are talking to a colleague at work. There has been a problem over ordering some computer software. Your colleague was not specific about when you needed to place the order, and the software has not arrived. Your colleague becomes quite angry. Your feelings are very hurt by his behavior, and you feel quite emotional.
3. You are married. It's 1:00 a.m., and you have just returned home after going out with some old friends. You have had a wonderful time. Your husband is still awake when you walk in the door.
4. You are out having a cup of coffee with a male friend you know through school. You feel very sad and depressed, but you don't know why. You woke up this morning feeling this way. You feel as if you could start crying for no reason.
5. You are in a car with your brother driving out of town. He is driving, and you are in the passenger seat. You are talking about a party that you went to last night, and suddenly you both realize that you are lost.
6. You are talking to one of your salespeople about his performance at work. This employee needs to improve in some areas. You are making direct suggestions for improvement hoping that your employee will sell more in the future.

Scenario Activities: Descriptions of Male Roles

1. You and your wife live in a very nice two-bedroom apartment. You both work, and you have enough money to live on, but you have school loans to pay and many other bills. Right now, the interest rate on home loans is very high, so you can't afford to buy a house.

2. You are talking to a colleague at work. Your colleague was supposed to order some computer software, which you need right now. The software has not arrived. You feel very angry with your colleague.

3. You are married. Your wife has gone out tonight with some friends. It is now 1:00 a.m., and she has just walked in the door.

4. You are out having a cup of coffee with a female friend you know through school. You want to tell her about a great movie that you just saw.

5. You are in a car with your sister driving out of town. You are talking about a party that you went to last night, and suddenly you both realize that you are lost.

6. You are talking to your supervisor about your performance as a salesperson at work. You do not agree with everything your supervisor has to say to you.

BOUNDARY ISSUES 2:
COUNTRY DESCRIPTIONS, CHAPTER 4, PAGES 97–98

Materialia

This country is a large military power, perhaps the greatest in the world, and thus has been heavily involved in world politics. Its area is very large, but its population is average in number. It has vast material resources, but because it uses great amounts of energy (the largest per capita consumption in the world), it relies heavily on imported energy supplies. Its government is very stable. Its economy is fairly strong but is showing recent signs of decline. Many believe that a major recession is on the way for **Materialia.**

Materialia's neighbor, **Brookland,** is poor, and its municipal services are of very low quality. **Brookland** does not have adequate sewage treatment plants. Much of its raw sewage is piped directly into a river that flows into **Materialia.** Also, many **Brooklandese** enter **Materialia** illegally to find work.

Roxbury, a country that **Materialia** has defended militarily in past decades, exports huge amounts of goods to **Materialia,** resulting in a large trade imbalance. The expected recession in **Materialia** is causing tensions between the two countries.

Waterland has long provided bases for **Materialia's** military, giving **Materialia** valuable strategic positions. Now many of **Waterland's** citizens are pressing for the removal of **Materialia's** military forces.

Cornopia is the country from which **Materialia** gets most of its energy supplies. In turn, **Materialia** has supplied **Cornopia** with vast quantities of military hardware. Now an internal uprising is showing weak but potentially hazardous signs of danger to the government of **Cornopia.**

Waterland

Waterland is a strong economic country with a long, proud history. It has a small self-defense force, but must rely on **Materialia** for the bulk of its protection. (**Materialia** is happy to do this, because **Waterland** provides an important strategic location.) **Waterland** does not have much in the way of energy resources, but thanks to heavy government subsidies, it has developed alternative fuel sources that keep it relatively free of dependence on imported energy. **Waterland's** economy is robust, showing only signs of continued healthy growth. Its trade with other nations is generally balanced.

Waterland has a very liberal policy regarding immigration. It has welcomed many migrant workers from **Brookland** and has provided these immigrants with good working and social conditions. Recently, however, because of racial differences between the two countries, the citizens of **Waterland** have pressured the government to stop this immigration.

Waterland severely restricts imports of goods from Roxbury. Roxbury's industries are heavy polluters, and acid rain is largely the result of Roxbury's factories. Waterland is the recipient of much of this acid rain.

Many of Waterland's citizens are pressing the government for the removal of Materialia's military. Waterland's government fears losing the support of the people if it does not give in to the citizens' demands.

Waterland has no extradition treaty with Cornopia. A notorious criminal from Waterland has sought refuge in Cornopia, and the government of Cornopia has refused to turn the criminal over. The government of Waterland strongly desires extradition of this criminal.

Cornopia

A large, enormously wealthy nation, Cornopia has gotten its wealth through development of huge deposits of energy. It exports this energy to virtually every country in the world, with the exception of Waterland. Surrounded by hostile neighbors, Cornopia has relied on Materialia to provide it with military hardware. Cornopia's government has been stable. Recent years have brought prosperity to its people, but there has been a slight, subtle suppression of human rights. As a result, a newly formed political movement is showing signs of being a threat to the government.

Cornopia has always had an uneasy relationship with Waterland. A man whom Waterland considers to be a criminal has fled to Cornopia. Cornopia considers him, if not innocent, benign. Cornopia, having tremendous wealth, has invested abroad heavily and has a fair amount of assets in Waterland.

Brookland, which borders Cornopia, has recently discovered large deposits of energy. Brookland wishes to develop these deposits, but doesn't have the technology it needs to do this. Some of the deposits may extend across the border into Cornopia.

Cornopia imports a great number of goods from Roxbury. Unfortunately, Roxbury's factories produce a large amount of pollution. Because Cornopia is downstream of a river that runs through Roxbury, Cornopia is feeling the impact of Roxbury's

waste material. Cornopia is considering raising the price of energy exports to Roxbury to pay for the clean up.

Roxbury

Roxbury is a medium-sized country that has become very prosperous. It has done this mostly through its vigorous export business. Roxbury has very few natural resources and must import almost all of its energy, mostly from Cornopia. Roxbury's government is very stable and enjoys the support of the people. Roxbury has a small military. It has relied on Materialia for its protection, but Roxbury has a long militaristic history and could be expected to raise substantial forces in a short amount of time if it desired. Roxbury is a manufacturing giant, but labor costs at home are beginning to soar.

Roxbury's main interest is in exporting its products. Many business leaders see a great but unexploited market in Brookland.

Roxbury has a large trade surplus with Materialia and has thus received pressure from Materialia to reduce exports. Roxbury, in turn, is worried about the declining health of Materialia's economy. Because Materialia is a major market for Roxbury's goods, a recession in Materialia would be disastrous for Roxbury's business.

As well as access to Brookland's market, Roxbury wants to get into the market in Waterland. Roxbury is very envious of Waterland's energy technology, which, if obtained, could greatly benefit Roxbury.

Cornopia has recently threatened to raise Roxbury's energy prices because of pollution concerns. Businesses in Roxbury believe Roxbury's pollution laws to be adequate and strongly oppose any move to make environmental laws stricter.

Brookland

Brookland is a poor country with a large, growing population and some big environmental problems. Brookland borders Waterland, Materialia, and Cornopia. Each year it loses some of its population through emigration to Waterland (legally) and to

Materialia (illegally). **Brooklandese** migrate to these two countries because work in their homeland is nearly impossible to find. This emigration breaks up families in a culture where the family is central in people's lives. **Brookland** has no military to speak of. Recently, large energy deposits have been found in an area bordering **Cornopia.** This could be a great source of wealth to **Brookland,** but it doesn't have the resources or the technology to develop these deposits.

Being a dry country, **Brookland** is always in need of water. **Brookland** has traditionally imported water from **Cornopia,** but this year that water has been unavailable due to the pollution of the main river in **Cornopia.**

Brooklandese working in **Waterland** have recently been harassed by citizens of **Waterland.** One has even been killed. **Brookland** believes that racism is behind this sudden surge of violence.

Emigration to **Materialia** for work is an important source of income for many **Brookland** families, but recently the government of **Materialia** has begun to control illegal immigration more tightly, with the result that fewer **Brooklandese** are able to work in **Materialia.**

The new leader of **Brookland** has promised to look abroad for economic assistance. He believes that without help from foreign countries, **Brookland** will never be able to pull itself up by its own bootstraps.

TRANSCRIPTS

CHAPTER 1: SCHOOL DAZE

Listening 1, page 10: Talking to an Advisor

Advisor: Hello, Soo-Jin, how are you doing?

Soo-Jin: Not very well. I was dropped from a class that I needed to take this semester.

Advisor: You were dropped from the class? What happened?

Soo-Jin: Well, this class was added at the last minute because there were so many students who needed it. I went to the class the first day it opened, and I thought that I would be added to the class because I was there that day. The professor said something about turning in the add slip right away, but I needed to get a signature for another class I was adding, so I waited.

Advisor: So you didn't turn in the add slip right away?

Soo-Jin: Right. Then I got sick the next day and missed the class. The following day when I went in to class, the teacher announced that anyone who had not turned in an add slip or missed any classes had been dropped. She said that there were too many students who wanted to take the class, and she had to accept the students who had added and were attending.

Advisor: So what did you do at that point?

Soo-Jin: I left the class because I was so upset. I really needed that class to fulfill my requirements, and now my plans are ruined.

Listening 2, page 13: Real People/Real Voices: Alex's and Sheva's Experiences

Alex: Don't you just hate the beginning of the semester, Sheva?

Sheva: Yeah . . . the beginning of the semester always makes me kind of crazy. Things get so frustrating and confusing if I don't do everything I need to do, and even then, things may not work out the way I thought they would.

Alex: Yeah, usually I try to prepare myself and take care of all the details so I have as few surprises as possible. I'd rather be overprepared than underprepared. Like I get really frustrated if I can't add a class that I need. So, if I want to add a class, I get there early for the teacher's signature.

Sheva: Right. That's what I do. Then, if the teacher lets me into the class, I immediately turn in my add slip so that I'm registered in the class.

Alex: Yeah, I try to do that as soon as I can. There are so many details, and if you forget something, it causes a lot of problems.

Sheva: If the teacher says there's no room in the class, I get really anxious, but I don't give up. I usually go to the teacher's office and ask if I can be added to the class.

Alex: That's smart. It's so important to take it one step at a time so you don't feel like it's too much. Another thing I do is I always buy my books right away so I can look at them before the class starts. Then I don't feel so overwhelmed by the class when I get there.

Sheva: I buy my books early too. The lines at the bookstore are so long it can drive you crazy. So I always start reading the textbooks so I'm not wasting my time.

Alex: The first day of class is really important because that's when you find out about the work for the semester. That's when I decide if I'm going to stay in the class or drop it. Once classes begin and I've taken care of all the details, I feel much better.

Sheva: That's for sure.

Listening 3, page 20: The Introductory Lecture

Good morning. Today is the first class of English 400, and I'd like to go over some of the objectives and requirements for this class. Before I actually get into that, however, I'm going to talk a bit about this level and what it means to be in English 400. This class is the last class in the sequence before you're eligible for the composition class—English 1A. Because of that, by the end of this class, you have to demonstrate that your language skills make you capable of passing English 1A without too much difficulty. So . . . the standards for this class are quite high, and you'll have to make significant progress in your reading and writing skills in order to pass.

O.K. . . . so . . . now that I've given you that background, let's talk about some of the objectives and requirements for the class. The most important objective is to improve your reading and writing skills so that you can read a variety of texts and respond to them in writing. We will be reading fiction as well as nonfiction work. In writing, we will be working on your paraphrasing, summarizing, and essay-writing skills. We will also work on advanced grammar skills that apply especially to writing. During these first few weeks, we will be focusing on library research skills so that you will be prepared to do a longer research paper in the library later in the semester. You should come to class every day prepared for discussion on the reading assignment, and during class it is very important that you participate in the discussion. Later, the ideas that come up in the reading and discussions will be used for composition assignments. We will have regular in-class graded assignments, and you will turn in a portfolio of your work at the end of the semester. The evaluation criteria is on the syllabus, so if you have any questions about that, be sure to ask me.

Now that you understand the basic objectives and requirements for this class, let me say that if you work hard and really participate in class, you will make progress and enjoy the class. Remember, our goal is to improve reading and writing skills, so we're going to be reading quite a variety of stories, articles, and essays, and you'll have frequent opportunities to write. Finally, if you have any questions about anything on the syllabus, please see me during my office hours.

CHAPTER 2: WALKING A MILE IN ANOTHER PERSON'S MOCCASINS

Listening 1, page 35: Listen for the Language

Speaker A: Hey, I'm hungry. How about you? Did you eat yet?

Speaker B: No, I haven't eaten yet.

Speaker A: I was thinking about something ethnic. Do you like Thai food?

Speaker B: Yeah, I guess it's OK. Do you like it?

Speaker A: Yeah, and I know a great place downtown. You ever been to Thai Heaven?

Speaker B: No, I don't think I have.

Speaker A: Yeah, the prices are really reasonable and the food's great—really authentic. How does that sound to you?

Speaker B: Hmmm, I don't know, I guess that sounds all right.

Speaker A: OK, so do you want me to pick you up?

Speaker B: Oh, I don't want you to go to any trouble. It's not on your way.

Speaker A: It's no trouble at all. How does eight o'clock sound?

Speaker B: I guess that's fine. I think it's OK.

Speaker A: OK. Great! See you then.

The Sound of It, page 36: Reductions in Conversation

True Speech	Reduced Speech
1. Did you eat yet?	1. J'ya eetyet?
2. Do you like Thai food?	2. Ya like Thai food?
3. You ever been to Thai Heaven?	3. Y'ever been to Thai Heaven?
4. How does that sound to you?	4. Howzat sound to ya?
5. So, do you want me to pick you up?	5. So, d'ya want me to pick y'up?

Listening 2, page 40: Real People/Real Voices: Tamara's and Kirk's Experiences

Tamara:

I taught in Seoul, Korea, and I thought I had prepared myself pretty well with all the necessary travel books and my helpful Korean American roommate. I was really excited about teaching, 'cuz it was one of my first paying jobs as a teacher. I began each class by introducing myself, and I could see the excitement in my student's faces as they encountered a "real" California girl. Their enthusiasm made me feel so comfortable that I let them ask me some questions. To my amazement, I was confronted with a barrage of very personal questions.

"How old are you?"

"Are you married?"

"Why aren't you married?"

"Why did you come to Korea?"

I was really shocked and overwhelmed! I couldn't believe that the students could ask such personal questions and expect honest answers! After this happened in several classes, I realized there must be some cultural rule I was missing. The first thing I did was to stop giving the students the opportunity to ask me these questions, and the second was to find out why they thought these questions were appropriate.

I later found out that these questions are considered acceptable in Korea because age and marriage are used to establish status, and this is not information that is considered private or personal. Because of the close ties of family relationships in Korea, my students were concerned that I had traveled so far and left my family behind. Once I realized that there was culture and genuine concern at play, I felt much more comfortable about my first experiences, but in my year-long stay I no longer gave my students the opportunity to ask those questions.

Kirk:

The ten different language schools I attended in Mexico were much less sophisticated than where I teach in San Diego. Typically, students would stay with the same teacher for all of the half-day class. Class sizes were also smaller, with most ratios about 5:1. This made for a very informal atmosphere, where a lot of nicknames and first names were used. Maybe a more typical Mexican classroom at the high school and college level would have a more formal structure.

I was *amazed* by the liberalness—is that a word?—of teacher-initiated conversations. Drugs, religion, sexual issues were all discussed in a very open format. At first, I was afraid to talk about topics that are prone to "label" people here in the U.S., but after a while I became more comfortable, and then I really enjoyed joining in the conversations.

CHAPTER 3: I UNDERSTAND EXACTLY WHAT I THINK YOU SAID!

Listening 1, page 68: Gender Stereotypes
Dialogue 1: "The New Haircut"

Woman: Honey, do you notice anything different?

Man: Uhmmm, is that a new dress?

Woman: Nooo, I can't believe you can't tell!

Man: Uhmmm, I know! You got a haircut!

Woman: Yeah, how do you like it?

Man: Uhmmm, well, I guess it's OK.

Woman: Okay? What do you mean OK? Good OK or bad OK?

Man: It's OK; I mean it's OK.

Woman: Well, if you just think it's OK you must not like it.

Man: That's not what I said.

Woman: Well, then, what do you mean?

Man: Nothing, I don't mean anything!

Woman: I knew it. You really hate it, don't you?

Man: I didn't say that.

Woman: Yeah, but I know when you don't say anything good, it means you don't like it. I shouldn't have done it. I know you like my hair longer.

Man: It's only a haircut, and I think it looks fine.

Dialogue 2: "The Cocktail Bar Job Discussion"

Man: It's so great to finally meet you. I've heard a lot about you. Bob tells me you're majoring in social work.

Woman: Yeah, and what is it that you're studying exactly?

Man: I'm studying law. I'm going to specialize in immigration law.

Woman: That must be so fascinating.

Man: It really is. One of the best things is that I get to make so many important contacts. Just a couple of weeks ago I met with a group of immigration lawyers in Washington. There were hearings about the latest proposition. Have you ever been to Washington?

Woman: Well, as a matter of fact, I was there for a couple of days last summer. I attended meetings on the welfare to work program.

Man: The welfare program, hmmm, yes, one of my professors is recommending that I write a paper on those changes since it's so closely connected to immigration. He thinks I have a very good understanding of the program.

Woman: That's wonderful. I think it's so important to be encouraged by your professors. My professors have also been very supportive of my work. One of them is helping me to apply for a scholarship to graduate school.

Man: Oh, you're actually applying to graduate school? I guess you must be very motivated. I just got accepted to law school with a full scholarship. Once I get through that, I'll be on the road to success. That should show 'em I've made it.

Woman: Hmmm, I don't really look at it that way. I just want to have enough to provide for the things I care about.

Man: Not for me. I think the best part of success is having other people know you're successful.

Dialogue 3: "I Can Handle It Myself!"

Man: Are you having a good day at school today?

Woman: I guess so. I'm just feeling a little frustrated about the way Jim behaves, though.

Man: Why is that?

Woman: He has trouble getting all his papers done on time, so he's always asking for my help.

Man: That's easy. Just tell him no.

Woman: I feel upset because I want to be a nice person, but I just don't always have time to help him. I have a lot of work of my own.

Man: Tell him that. It's his work. It's not your responsibility.

Woman: He's such a nice man, and I really enjoy working with him. I wish I knew what to do.

Man: I've been telling you what to do. Just tell the guy you're not going to do his work for him anymore.

Woman: I'm not asking you what I should do . . . I just want you to understand that this is difficult for me.

Man: If you don't want to solve the problem, why did you bring it up?

Dialogue 4: "Do You Always Have to Cry?"

Woman: I'm home. The movie was so great; I'm sorry you didn't come with us.

Man: Uh-huh. Maybe next time.

Woman: I just love Larry Livingstone. Don't you think he's a great actor?

Man: I'm watching TV.

Woman: I know, but you just wouldn't believe how this movie touched me. It was so powerful.

Man: What's wrong with you? Can't you see that I'm watching the game? Can't we talk about the movie later?

Woman: I didn't mean to bother you. I just wanted to tell you about the movie. (*starts crying*)

Man: Do you need to get upset? I just asked you to wait. Is that so unreasonable?

Woman: No, but . . .

Man: Why do you always have to cry? I hate that.

Listening 2, page 70: Real People/Real Voices: Marty's, Sharon's, and Chris's Experiences

Marty's Problem:

Interviewer: So, Marty, I understand you're married. I was wondering what kinds of communication problems you have with your husband.

Marty: The first problem is that he doesn't answer directly—he beats around the bush. Like when I ask him a question about something, he won't give me specific information, and that makes me angry. And I don't get mad very easily. For example, he was having some problems with his business. I asked him about the situation, but he wouldn't tell me. I knew he was losing money, but he wouldn't tell me how much. Another problem is his reactions to my appearance. He thinks I'm beautiful, pretty, as long as I don't bother him. For example, he sits in front of the computer every day, and I come to him and ask, "How do I look?" And he'll tell me I look nice. But maybe I don't feel comfortable with what I'm wearing, so I go and change. I come back and ask him again, and he says the same thing: "Oh, you look good." He's not really paying attention, so maybe I'll go change again until I get it right. We're very different. He's very reserved, and I'm very open.

Sharon's Problem:

Interviewer: So, Sharon, I know you're not married, but you do have a boyfriend, so maybe you could tell me about some of the communication problems that you and your boyfriend have.

Sharon: OK, well I live in L.A., and my boyfriend lives in San Diego. So the only way we have to communicate is by telephone. And I'm a person who likes to talk a lot. He's a person who doesn't like to talk very much at all. So when I call him, I want to talk for a long time and tell him all about my day. And he doesn't really want to talk. So I will tell stories, and his only response will be, "Uh-huh!" "OK!" And I expect him to make comments and tell me his stories. So for me it is a little disappointing when I talk to him on the phone because I miss him, I want to hear a little bit more about what's happening in his life, and he doesn't tell me.

Interviewer: That sounds pretty difficult.

Sharon: It is difficult.

Interviewer: Do you ever tell him that you don't like that?

Sharon: Yes, I told him, and he said he would like to talk three times a day for five minutes instead of once a day for an hour. But I prefer to talk just in the evenings for a long time.

Chris's Problem:

Interviewer: OK. Chris, could you tell me a little bit about the communication problems you've experienced?

Chris: I was involved with a woman quite a while ago, and we were romantically involved. And at one time, a very important time, I was supposed to make a flight to a city in the Midwest, to Chicago, specifically. And unfortunately for me, I missed my flight—the flight that I was supposed to make to be there at the time that I told her to pick me up. And, as a result of that, she went to the airport, and when the flight arrived, I wasn't on it. And I tried to call her when I had a layover before the flight reached its destination, and I was unable to get in touch with her. So, as a result she arrived at the airport, and when the flight arrived, I wasn't on it. And she was upset about it, and I understood that she was upset about it. But she also should've understood that these things happen, and not to be so upset about it. This was quite some time ago, so the very specific details I don't recall, but I do recall that shortly after that our relationship ended.

CHAPTER 4: CROSSING THE LINE

Listening 1, page 87: Listen for Intent

1. Adolfo and Tri are classmates.

   Adolfo: Excuse me, Tri. Did you bring your book today?

   Tri: Yes, I did. Why?

   Adolfo (*polite/soft tone*): I forgot my book today, and we're going to review for the quiz. Would you mind sharing your book with me while we do the review?

2. Richard and Sandra are officemates.

   Richard: Hi, Sandra.

   Sandra: Hi, Richard.

   Richard: How are you doing?

   Sandra (*irritated/demanding tone*): I'm OK, but you know I have to say, I'm a little irritated. You took the computer out of the office yesterday for your seminar, and I was stuck here with no computer. I'd really appreciate it if you'd let me know in the future if you want to take the computer out of the office.

3. Mr. Sarkis and Ms. Arawan are negotiating at a peace conference.

> **Ms. Arawan:** Well, Mr. Sarkis, that's what we can offer you. I think you'll agree that it is a very generous offer. So perhaps we can sign the agreement now?
>
> **Mr. Sarkis (*strong/demanding tone*):** It would help us if you gave us more time to speak with our council members about these negotiations before we reach a final decision.

4. Lucia and Christina are business partners.

> **Lucia:** This proposal is ready to be signed. I'm glad we finished it before the end of the week.
>
> **Christina:** Me too! That was a lot of work, but I think we did a good job.
>
> **Lucia:** Yes, I think so too. (*polite/soft tone*) Listen, would you mind doing the final revisions while I go meet with the sales team?

5. Bill and Sonja are in the same cohort group working on a final project for a graduate seminar.

> **Bill:** Well, the group is almost finished with this project, but we're still waiting for the data that you were supposed to gather.
>
> **Sonja:** Yes, I know, but I've had three tests this week, and I'm feeling really overloaded right now.
>
> **Bill (*polite/soft tone*):** I understand, but as you know this project is due very soon. We could sure use those statistics by Friday so that we don't miss the deadline.

Listening 2, page 91: Conflict Resolution

Today we are going to discuss the steps involved in mediation counseling. The skills that make up mediation counseling will be useful to you in a variety of situations, for instance helping a couple that is having problems in their relationship or parents who are having trouble with a teenager. So often people think that getting angry at someone, and just telling them, will help to solve a problem. That simply is not true. In fact, often it can make a conflict worse. Through mediation counseling people can learn to take a series of steps that will lead them to identify problems and create solutions. However, as a counselor the most important thing for you to remember is that if you have people in front of you who have willingly come for help, you are halfway to solving the conflict. Let's run through the steps now.

Step One: Setting Up a Positive Environment

In step one the mediator wants to set up an environment that will help the clients to speak frankly about what has upset them without attacking the other person. This is first done by clearly stating specific rules about how the clients will be allowed to behave during mediation sessions. For example, clients must treat each other with respect. They may not shout at the other person or interrupt them when they are speaking. After the rules have been established, each client will take a turn speaking directly to the mediator. They will state their point of view concerning the problem. If they are having difficulty, the mediator will facilitate the process by asking questions like "What's been going on between the two of you?" or "How has this problem affected you?" Another thing the mediator will do is rephrase statements that sound very aggressive and accusatory. For example, if Robert is mad at Vicky, he might say something like this: "The problem is Vicky's always late. She has no respect for my time. She always keeps me waiting." To avoid having Vicky get angry when she hears this, the mediator would rephrase it, focusing on the real issue instead of on how bad Vicky is. The mediator might say something like this: "So you feel really frustrated and impatient when you arrive promptly and then have to wait a long time for the other person." When both clients have finished sharing their side of the story with the mediator, the mediator will list and clarify the problems. In the case of Robert and Vicky the mediator could say, "There seems to be a problem finding a way to organize time that is comfortable for both of you."

Step Two: Identifying the Bottom Line

In step two, the mediator helps the clients identify the bottom line. This is done by breaking their conflict down into specific issues which are emotional and behavioral. People might say they are mad about a specific behavior, but what they are really mad about is how it makes them feel. To look again at the case of Robert and Vicky, the mediator might help them to see that while time seems to be the issue, the real issue is that Robert feels Vicky does not respect him, because she does not honor her spoken commitment. She doesn't follow through on what she says to him. So the content issue here is that they disagree about how to organize time. Robert is prompt and has to wait, while Vicky is frequently late. The emotional issue is that this problem makes Robert feel that Vicky has no respect for him or for his time. At this point the clients begin speaking to each other. But they do this by participating in activities that are designed to help them better understand each other. Maybe they could do a role reversal, and Vicky could talk about how she would feel if she and Robert were supposed to have dinner with friends and he came an hour late. Robert could share reasons why he might be late for something. The mediator can also ask Robert and Vicky questions like "How do you think you would feel in this situation" or "Have you ever been in a similar situation?" Hopefully this will help Robert and Vicky be more sympathetic with one another.

Step Three: Brainstorming

Now it's time to talk about solutions. In step three, the mediator encourages the clients to share every possible solution to their problem no matter how ridiculous or extreme. The clients must accept all the solutions either one of them suggests. They may not criticize each other during this step in the process. As they are making suggestions, the mediator writes down all their different ideas. When everyone has run out of suggestions, they look at their list. They try to identify which solution is best, which one is most reasonable or practical, which ones are unworkable, etc. etc. They prioritize the solutions and discuss which ones would work for them, which ones they would be willing to try.

Step Four: Writing a Shared Commitment

Using the solutions they have chosen, the clients, with the help of the mediator, write down some very specific steps they would take to solve their problem. They do this without blaming each other. For example, Robert and Vicky might write a statement that says "We agree that if either one of us is going to be more than fifteen minutes late, we will call and tell our partner what's happening so that they won't wonder where we are and when we're coming home." OR "If one of us is more than fifteen minutes late, then the other has the right to assume that the appointment is off and to make other plans." OR "We agree that instead of always going in one car to social occasions, we can take separate cars and each arrive when it's convenient for us."

Conclusion

Those are the four steps we go through when dealing with conflict. They may seem very obvious, and in fact you may be aware of times when you have done the things described in each step. But the point of mediation counseling is to help facilitate this process between people who are either too angry or don't have these skills to sit down and deal with their problems in an organized, structured, positive way. Now before we apply what we've learned, does anyone have any questions?

Listening 3, page 94: Real People/Real Voices: Doo-Won's and Katica's Experiences

Doo-Won, would you like a world with no boundaries? And what would you say to world leaders about this?

Doo-Won: Well as you know, my country, Korea, is divided into two parts—the North and the South. Of course, I don't like this because we are really all one people and one country. So if I could talk to the government leaders about this situation, this is what I would say: You know, you guys, would you mind getting rid of that boundary between North and South Korea? I don't want my country to be divided into two parts anymore. We all speak the same language, and we have the same culture. I'd really appreciate it if I could travel to the northern part of my own country. I have the right to see my whole country, not just half of it. The people in the north are just suffering because of this boundary anyway. Many people are starving up there. It would help them if you came to an agreement and reunified the country again. Look at other parts of the world. Look at the Eastern Bloc and the way they took the wall down. We could sure use some wise politicians who would take our wall down. Yes, I would like a world with no boundaries, and I'd appreciate it if we could start in my own country.

Katica, would you like a world with no boundaries? And what would you say to world leaders about this?

Katica: Yeah, I would like it if there were no more boundaries in the world. So if I could talk to the world leaders I would say this. I'd really appreciate it if you could stop creating wars about boundaries. I come from the former Yugoslavia, where there has been a lot of fighting over boundaries. Would you mind making an agreement so that we don't have any more of this fighting? It doesn't matter if a person is a Serb or a Croatian. We can all live together in the same country like we used to. We could sure use some good negotiating to take care of these problems. There are too many dangerous people in power. I had to leave my country because of all these problems. I can't even live in my own country because of all these boundary problems. It would help if you leaders spent more time trying to solve these problems.

CHAPTER 5: MY SLICE OF THE PIE

Listening 1, page 104: Real People/Real Voices: Grace's Experience

Q: Do you think people today do a good job of planning for financial emergencies?

A: Well, I think most people want to have a secure future. Um, however, the information they need, um, to achieve financial security isn't at their fingertips. Um, OK, for example, well, they need to establish their goals, for instance, how much money do you need to live, what would be a basic amount that you need to live? They have to take things like whether they want to pay for their children to go to college, which college they're going to go to, um, and many people in the baby boomer group are faced with having to care for a parent, which is an added expense and has to be, um, considered in any future financial decision.

Q: Then how much money do you think people need to save for themselves?

A: Well, the thing is, you should have 3–6 months of monthly salary saved, so whatever your monthly salary is you should have enough to pay your expenses for 3–6 months without any income.

Q: And then in addition to that, most of us need to plan for college, retirement, taking care of parents, etc.?

A: Uh-huh. And the kinds of things that rise up unexpectedly, for example, like the water heater blowing up or the car not starting in the morning.

Q: So, what's the biggest mistake people make?

A: Well, they tend to live from paycheck to paycheck. And when something unexpectedly occurs, if they don't have someone to help, they just go deeper and deeper into debt, you fall farther and farther behind in your payments. Or, it gets so bad that you lose everything, like what has happened to many people who are forced into homelessness and are there because their debts became overwhelming.

Q: So, if you could give people one piece of advice to make their financial future more secure, what would you suggest?

A: Younger people often spend every last cent that they earn. They live from paycheck to paycheck. After they pay their bills, they complain that there's nothing left over to save. The best advice I can give is to say "Pay yourself first." When you get your paycheck, save some portion of it, even $10 a week. That's giving up a movie, and one stop at a fast food restaurant. Let's say you start with $3000, and you add $10 a week to that at a pretty reasonable rate of 13% a year. In 60 years you'll have 5.6 million dollars. That's pretty amazing, isn't it?

Listening 2, page 115: The Cost of Education

A: I'm really worried about paying my tuition for the next term at school. School fees are getting so high. I may have to cut back on my classes and work more hours to earn more.

B: *I understand that you* worry about that. Every year *it seems to me* that more students worry about money.

A: I agree. And it's hard to study full time and hold down any kind of job.

B: *Have you thought about* applying for financial aid?

A: Ya know, I have, but *the real problem is that* so many people apply and there's just not enough financial aid available.

B: *Maybe you could* qualify for some kind of student loan that you would repay after you finish studying. *You should* go to the financial aid office and see what the requirements are.

A: I suppose that's true. Sometimes I wish the cost of education was completely covered by the government. It would sure make my life easier.

B: Maybe, but somebody would still be paying for it. Just not you right now. And I sure don't want to pay higher taxes to cover the cost.

A: *The real problem is that* you just can't give everybody what they want. More services always means more taxes.

B: Don't you think that's true everywhere, and in a lot of different situations? I'm sure we're not the only ones who are worried about this.

A: *Oh, I think it's quite clear that* a lot of people think about this. And with a good education be-

coming more and more necessary to get a good job, I think more people will worry in the future. I can't even pay for myself! How am I supposed to save up to pay for my kids to go to school?

B: Hey, when you find the answer to that one, be sure to tell me. You could make a lot of money selling that piece of advice.

The Sound of It, page 116:
Guessing Meaning from Intonation

1. I'm *really* worried about paying my tuition for the next term at school. School fees are getting *so* high.
2. It's *hard* to study full time and hold down any kind of job.
3. You just *can't* give *everybody* what they want.
4. Don't you think that's true *everywhere,* and in a *lot* of different situations?
5. I'm *sure* we're not the *only* ones who are worried about this.
6. Oh, I think it's *quite* clear that a *lot* of people worry about this.
7. I can't even pay for *myself!* How am I supposed to pay for my *kids* to go to school?
8. Hey, when you find the answer to *that* one, be sure to tell me. You could make a lot of money selling *that* piece of advice.

CHAPTER 6: I SAID IT MY WAY

Listening 1, page 131: The V-Chip Debate

Lawyer: In my opinion, one of the most important freedoms people can have is the freedom to say, read, write, or watch whatever they want to. As an attorney, I want to work to protect this freedom. The v-chip prevents people from being able to watch whatever they want, and I strongly believe that the v-chip is a form of censorship. I think this is wrong.

Parent: Of course I also feel that freedom is an important right. But installing v-chips in televisions is not about freedom or censorship. It's not about preventing adults from watching what-

ever they want to. Looking at this as a parent, I believe installing v-chips in televisions is a way to protect our children from seeing too much violence and too much sex on TV at an early age, when these children probably aren't ready to decide for themselves what is good or bad for them to watch. That's a choice parents need to make.

Lawyer: In my point of view, parents can already control this. Parents can already prevent their kids from seeing inappropriate programs simply by changing the channel. Nothing could be easier.

Parent: I have to disagree. It's well-known that people are watching more television than ever, especially children. It's a fact that the average child now watches an average of four hours of television a day, and for many busy parents, television is a way to keep the kids busy while the parents cook, clean, and take care of other household chores. And it's simply a fact that parents don't always watch television with their kids, so they need a way to control the programs even if the parent is not there.

Lawyer: I believe that's an issue of what it means to be a responsible parent. Most child-care experts strongly recommend that parents make the effort to watch TV with their kids. If they do, seeing some sexual content or violence becomes something parents and kids can talk about together, an opportunity for discussion, an opportunity to learn. Using television as an opportunity for discussion and learning is a much better choice than simply censoring certain programming.

Parent: I'm positive that parents should watch television with their kids as often as they can. However, in my opinion, expecting parents to always be there to supervise what their kids watch, to answer questions and discuss ideas, is not practical or possible for most families. V-chip technology makes it possible for parents to have greater control, and that's a good thing.

Listening 2, page 138: Real People/Real Voices: Bruce's Experience

Actually, uh, as a journalist I don't think the media should be prying into the private lives of public figures, um, especially if those actions are not criminal. Obviously, if the public figure has, uh, committed a felony or murdered someone, we, the public should, uh, should know about that. But for extramarital affairs or consensual activities I would say no.

Um, I think the real measure as to whether to publish a story or not should be the motivation. In other words, is it being, uh, published solely to increase the sale of newspapers, or enhance the popularity of the journalist? Or is it being published because it's a genuine subject of national interest and concern?

I admit there will be issues where intelligent people, mmm, disagree about which side of this an issue falls on, but other issues will be easier to decide. Maybe a measure can be, if this were to be published about a candidate you support, would you honestly want to go ahead with the story?

The Sound of It, page 139: Conversational Pauses

1. Really? Hmm. I read a newspaper every day. (pause to show the idea is unexpected)
2. Mmm. Actually, I get a lot of helpful information from using the Internet in the campus computer lab. (pause to show disagreement)
3. I think, uh, watching television is a pretty good way to improve my English. (pause to show time is needed to think)
4. Mmm. We need to have a lot more newspapers and magazines available in the library. (pause to show disagreement)
5. I, um, don't like it that the news on TV shows so much, um, graphic violence nowadays. (pause to show that time is needed to think)

CHAPTER 7: IT'S NOT EASY BEING GOOD

The Sound of It, page 153: Correct Stress Placement

We live in a transition period, when the old faiths which comforted nations, and not only so, but made nations, seem to have spent their force. I do not find the religions of men at this moment very creditable to them. . . . The fatal trait is the divorce between religion and morality. Here are know-nothing religions or churches that proscribe intellect; . . . the lover of the old religion complains that our contemporaries, scholars as well as merchants, succumb to a great despair . . . and believe in nothing. In our large cities, the population is godless . . . no bond, no fellow-feeling, no enthusiasm. There are not men, but hungers, thirsts, fevers, and appetites walking. How is it people manage to live on,—so aimless as they are?

—Ralph Waldo Emerson

(pause)

1. transition
2. creditable
3. proscribe
4. contemporaries
5. succumbed
6. despair
7. aimless

(slight pause)

8. divorce
9. morality
10. complain
11. enthusiasm
12. population
13. comforted
14. nations
15. fatal
16. intellect
17. scholars
18. merchants
19. nothing
20. godless
21. hunger
22. fever
23. appetite

Listening 1, page 156: Real People/Real Voices: Chris's Experience

When I was a small schoolboy, um, the motto of our school was "Do It Because It's Right," and what I have been doing since then, that motto had been lingering with me; um, I was searching for a philosophical and a spiritual framework that incorporated these ethics without getting hung up in a dogma of worshipping a divine figure, um, I could never buy into a Christian ideal of a divine spirit, um, that would judge, um, our foibles and our failures and our successes. Um, I have always believed that those judgments, um, were best left to the individual and that there was always a chance for redemption, not from some higher figure but actually from your own actions. Buddhism is one philosophy and practice that helps me to be aware of my own failures and helps me be aware of how to re-, continually repent and continually address um, you know, mistakes I might make in treating other people. It also helps me understand the idea of causation and how my actions affect others, and how a single reaction from one individual will affect another individual's reaction, and, uh, that brings home the importance of having correct speech, correct actions, correct intentions, um, and correct wisdom in dealing with situations and with other people. I think it's very important to deal with people and give them joy and hope and confidence and compassion in every circumstance, um, because that helps carry them along, um, and helps make the world in a very small way a much better place. Um, I can always be a better person, and Buddhism helps me reflect on that so I can be a better person. It shows me that my compassion for other human beings can be without limits, and the only limits that exist are ones that I set myself. And it always, it goes back to that motto that stuck in me to "Do It Because It's Right," and if I have a framework where I can check my actions and check my intentions and check how I behave with other people, I can always make sure that I do it because it's right, and that's why I am an avid practitioner.

Listening 2, page 161: Listen for the Language

Dialogue 1: Alternative Pain Medicine

Doctor: How are you doing with the pain so far, Mr. Martin? There's often a lot of pain associated with this stage of cancer.

Patient: It's pretty bad. The medication you've given me doesn't seem to help much.

Doctor: Well, there are alternative methods, but we haven't talked much about them.

Patient: Alternative methods? What do you mean?

Doctor: In some cases, marijuana has been used to help with pain for cancer patients.

Patient: Marijuana! But that's a drug! **Do you mean to say that you actually** recommend an illegal drug to your patients? **It's inconceivable to me that** anyone could use drugs.

Doctor: **It's possible that I would** recommend marijuana, especially if I thought I could prevent real suffering. In your case, small amounts of marijuana could do a lot to stop your pain.

Patient: **I would never even consider smoking marijuana.** Not even in this situation.

Doctor: I certainly understand how you feel. Using marijuana in this situation is a big step. There are some books I can recommend. Maybe if you read them and get some more information about many different forms of alternative pain relief, you'll find something that feels comfortable to you.

Patient: I'd like to learn more. Even if I choose not to use marijuana, **it's possible that I would consider using other alternative methods.**

Doctor: Good. On the way out, just ask the receptionist for the book list.

Dialogue 2: What's Best for Grandmother

A: Now that Grandma has broken her hip, she's going to need extra care, even after she recovers.

B: Yeah, I know. She really shouldn't live alone anymore, but I'm worried that we don't have the time or resources to take care of her.

A: **One thing we might do** is start looking for a good nursing home.

B: **If we** put her into a nursing home, **I would** feel absolutely terrible. We live right here in the same city! Don't you think she might feel that we just don't care?

A: Well, maybe we could find a nursing home that's very close to one of our houses. That way, we could arrange to go over every couple of days, even if it's just for a few minutes.

B: **Hmm, I never thought** of looking for a nursing home that close. **Isn't it difficult to** think of putting her in one of those places?

A: Of course it's difficult. But I want her to have good medical care and a lot of attention, and we both work all day. I don't see any other solutions.

CHAPTER 8: SCIENTIFICALLY SPEAKING

The Sound of It, page 170: Using Intonation to Emphasize Different Points of View

1. On the **one** hand, it **is** important to test products for safety before selling them, but on the **other** hand, you can't deny that many animals have to suffer terribly in order for these products to be tested.
2. **One** way of looking at it is to say technology can be very dangerous, but **another** way of looking at it is to recognize that the technology is **neutral**. It's **people** who make it dangerous when they use it in harmful ways.
3. Yes, I supposed you **could** say that e-mail saves a lot of time at work. You could **also** say that communication through computers eliminates important human contact that builds important relationships.

4. I guess you're **right** that computers are very helpful and useful for students, but you **can't ignore** that some students spend so much time on their computers that they don't develop other necessary life skills.

Listening 1, page 174: Seeing Both Sides

Host: Good morning, and welcome to today's broadcast of *Seeing Both Sides*. Today we have something very interesting for you—a very controversial topic. Is it a moral use of technology to take advantage of fetal tissue for medical experimentation? Our guests today are Dr. Kim Benson, head of the Organization of Physicians for Responsible Research, and the Reverend William Cooper. They're here to discuss the moral and medical implications of this new area of research.

Good morning, Doctor and Reverend. Dr. Benson, let's begin by hearing the arguments in favor.

Dr. Benson: Well, scientifically speaking, it's clear that fetal tissue is quite a gold mine. It's been proven to be extremely successful in grafting new tissue for use with burn victims. Research is being done into other potential uses as well.

Host: Reverend Cooper, how do you respond to that? What about these benefits?

Reverend Cooper: Well, of course I see the doctor's point, and it is extremely important to do everything possible in terms of research to alleviate human suffering; however, you can't ignore the fact that fetal tissue is a product of abortion, which many consider to be an act of murder. Just as we hope you would not kill another person to benefit yourself, it is immoral to use the life of a fetus in this way.

Dr. Benson: Yes, Reverend Cooper, I suppose some people could say abortion is an act of murder, but it's really important to clearly separate issues here. You can't ignore the fact that abortion is legal in this country at this time. Certainly, while we may recognize that as a grave human tragedy, it is a fact that it happens frequently, thousands of times every day. If this is the case, it makes good medical sense to derive any benefit from it that we can. Isn't the tragedy perhaps minimized if this tissue can be used to further human life? And, indeed, in terms of using this tissue to create new, healthy, living skin for burn victims, are we not in some small way allowing that life to continue?

Reverend Cooper: That's one way of looking at it. However, another way of looking at it is to say that the life of that fetus deserves every opportunity to grow and develop as an individual—that using these victims is simply adding insult to injury. And really, Dr. Benson, can you seriously mean to imply that the benefit this tissue provides for skin grafts for burn victims balances the fact that a human life and all its potential has been taken without its consent?

Dr. Benson: Maybe you have a point there, and I'm sure many people would agree with you, but the flip side of the issue is that our greatest moral obligation is to the living. As long as abortion is legal, as long as those fetuses are not developing into full-fledged human life, it seems we must devote our energies to concentrating on and helping in every way possible those who are alive and suffering.

Reverend Cooper: What exactly do you mean, Dr. Benson? Are you condoning abortion?

Dr. Benson: It doesn't matter whether or not I condone it. On one hand, we could spend a great deal of time arguing about abortion. On the other hand, that would be a waste of time since our opinions here don't change the fact that it is legal. We may as well accept the legality and go from there.

Host: You've both raised a number of very interesting points. I'm sure you've given our listeners a lot of food for thought about this complex and controversial issue. Let's take a short break now, and when we return we'll take some calls from our listeners.

Listening 2, page 180: Real People/Real Voices: Susana's Experience

When my husband and I first found out that we were going to have a baby, we were thrilled. But at my very first doctor's appointment I got kind of scared, because before I even had a physical examination the doctor set me up for an appointment for genetic counseling and a bunch of prenatal tests. I mean, I feel lucky to have good medical insurance and to be able to get good care while I'm pregnant, but it's scary to realize that it's now a normal part of many pregnancies to have all kinds of tests to find out the health of the baby very early on, to find out about possible birth defects and genetic diseases. I had a friend who just refused to have any of these tests. She said she just couldn't face the possibility of knowing that the baby might have a terrible defect, or a serious illness that meant the baby couldn't live, and then she might have to make some horrible, painful choices. She said she just wanted to go on with hope. I don't know how I feel about this. To think that the tests might find something that could be treated by doctors even before the baby is born and that I didn't make it possible for the doctors to do this seems horrible. To think that the tests might show that my child has a terrible birth defect or might not live after the birth is also horrible. I know the tests are supposed to help, but in a way they just make being pregnant that much harder because no matter what we decide to do, the consequences can be so serious and I'll always have to live with the results of my choice.

CHAPTER 9: THE NATURE OF THINGS— ENVIRONMENTAL CONCERNS

Listening 1, page 196: Discussing the Environment

Host: OK. Let's take another call. This is from Frank Grant, and he's calling from his car.

Grant: Yeah, Mr. Stevens, you said that one of the biggest problems we're facing is the way that technological advances are posing a threat to the environment. What concerns me is that you ignore the ways that technology can actually reverse some of this damage. It really bothers me when technology is seen as the major cause of environmental problems.

Stevens: Well, Mr. Grant, take a look at the invention of the automobile. Don't you see the impact this technological advance has had on the increase in air pollution and the depletion of the ozone layer? I'm very concerned about the irreversible damage that we see in changing weather patterns as well because of this and other modern innovations in technology.

Grant: Of course I see that, but look at the development that technology has made recently with the invention of an electric car that will no longer emit harmful pollutants. You aren't looking at the whole picture. Your argument represents a very narrow view, just like the argument that says overpopulation causes environmental problems. First of all, overpopulation can be limited by advances in science that create safer methods of birth control, and secondly, there are ways that science and technology can help to solve some of the problems of overpopulation. For example, to cut down on the pollution caused by so many people driving to work, we can develop more effective means of mass transit like high-speed commuter trains.

Stevens: I understand your point, Mr. Grant, but I just don't think that the technological solutions can keep up with the environmental damage that's being done. I intend to continue my fight against the negative impact of technology on the environment.

Listening 2, page 201: Real People/Real Voices: Chen's and Rafael's Experiences

Chen:

I know this sounds crazy, but the noisier it is, the better I study. Usually, if I have a test, I go to the student center and sit at a table, drink a cup of coffee, and study. Even though there are lots of students around talking and there's music playing in the background, I can concentrate pretty well. As a matter of fact, I usually get A's on tests if I study this way. Also, I like it better when I can sit in a comfortable chair, so if I'm at home, I sit in a recliner and it helps me to study for a longer period of time if I'm comfortable. If I do study at home, I usually wear my earphones and listen to music, which helps me to concentrate. That way, I don't get distracted and get up to do something around the house. It really doesn't help for me to try to study at the library because I feel so bored that it puts me to sleep. I need a lot of action and sound in my environment because it gives me energy to do my work.

Rafael:

Tests make me really nervous, so when I know I have a test coming, I find a very quiet place to study. I get distracted very easily, so I can't study when there are other people around or if there's music playing. I usually get C's on my tests, so it's important that I have the right environment and that I study hard. Sometimes I'll go to the library during the very early morning hours when it's actually silent because I can get a lot of work done in that environment. I also like to study at my desk in my room because I have all my books around and it inspires me to study hard. I have a good straight chair, which helps me to stay awake since I can't get too comfortable in it. The best time for me to study at home is at night because it's quiet and nobody is around. I can't concentrate if there is music playing or if people are talking around me because it really distracts me.

CHAPTER 10: ALL STRESSED OUT AND NO PLACE TO GO

Listen for the Language, page 211:
Techniques for Managing Stress

Host: Good morning, and welcome to *Talk of the Day*. Do you often find that you're trying to accomplish more in a day than is humanly possible? Do you have trouble falling asleep at night because you can't stop thinking about yesterday's activities or planning tomorrow's? Do you find yourself spending too much time at work without enough time for leisure activities? Today, our topic is stress and how to manage it. Tell us about the level of stress in your life and how you cope with it, or call us with your questions. With us to help answer some of the questions you may have is Dr. Elizabeth Sander, a medical doctor and writer of a best-selling book on stress management. She has also conducted numerous workshops designed to teach people how to identify and prevent stress. Good morning, Dr. Sander, and thank you for joining us today.

Dr. Sander: Thank you for having me.

Host: Dr. Sander, before we take our first call, perhaps you could just tell us exactly what we mean by "stress." We hear the word being used so much today. What is stress?

Dr. Sander: Yes, that's a very good question. Actually, stress can be either a physical or psychological response, or both, to the demands that we're placing on ourselves. An increased level of stress affects us physically by producing certain changes in the body such as increased heart or breathing rate, dilation of the pupils, or our blood pressure and sugar level can go up. These are normally responses that are designed to help us, for example, when we're in danger, but which under other circumstances, for example, when we have a deadline to meet for a project at work, don't really benefit us. Psychologically, we respond to these demands by becoming nervous, irritable, depressed, or even angry.

Host: Yes, it seems these days we're constantly listening to each other complain about being stressed out and feeling a variety of these responses which you've just mentioned. Well, let's see what kind of stress level our callers have. Let's take a call from Judy in Fallbrook.

Judy: Yes, hello, thank you for taking my call. This is a great topic. You know, I have so many friends who are always complaining about being stressed out. I just don't understand it. I just don't understand what it means to be stressed out. And it seems that I'm just as busy as they are if not more so. Maybe I'm really stressed and just don't realize it. Are there certain warning signs that I can be on the lookout for that will tell me I've reached a dangerous level of stress?

Dr. Sander: That's a great question, and yes, many people are at dangerous levels of stress without realizing it or they just don't want to admit it because they're afraid that they would have to change something in their life. Some of the most common warning signs are fatigue, listlessness, sleeping problems—either you can't fall asleep at night or you wake up throughout the night; you may have a loss of appetite or sudden stomach disorders, and heart palpitations are quite common. So one of the key issues is to help people realize that they are experiencing some of these problems associated with too much stress.

Judy: Well, as I said, many of my friends are aware of their situation, but it seems they never do anything about it. Are there ways that they can make their lives less stressful?

Dr. Sander: Of course. There are steps that we can take to lower the amount of stress in our lives, but unfortunately many people are so caught up in the cycle of activity and stress that they don't stop to take these important steps. The most important step is to become aware of potentially stressful situations and avoid them. We can also simply reduce our workload and organize the work that we do have in a better way. Another important step is to get the proper rest and exercise. If you're under a lot of stress to begin with, very often sleep or exercise can help to release some of that stress and prepare you to take on more. One of the worst things that can happen is to allow the stress to build up. Finally, one of the most effective steps we can take is to find a balance between work and play. In the U.S. it's been recently discovered that the average American is working more now than we did 20 years ago. We have become almost obsessed with work, and we have a hard time enjoying ourselves anymore.

Judy: Yeah, that's definitely true. Thank you. That information is really helpful.

Host: OK, let's take another call, from Lori in Ramona.

Lori: Hi, you know, I was listening to the previous caller, and for me it's not a problem of identifying the stress but what to do about it when it happens. I can't lower my workload right now, and I can't get more sleep because it would be impossible for me to get everything done if I did. It seems that when I get stressed out, I realize that I'm doing too much, and that makes me even more nervous.

Dr. Sander: Well, you seem to be a person that would benefit from a mental approach to stress management. Techniques such as visualization or meditation help many people who can't seem to make adjustments in their lives to lessen the amount of activity they're involved in. Having a more positive outlook or mentally planning your day's activities so that there will be less stress is also helpful.

Host: OK. We're going to take a short break, and when we return we'll hear more from Dr. Elizabeth Sander on the topic of stress.

Listening 1, page 219: Real People/Real Voices: Andrew's and Henry's Experiences

Andrew:

Interviewer: So, Andrew, I understand you've just finished your first college semester. Maybe you could tell me a little bit about some of the things that made you feel stressed out at college. And how did you deal with that?

Andrew: Well, um, one of the big things that stressed me out was there was a lot of, um, pressure on me from my parents and from myself to do well academically. And going there, I mean I haven't exactly had a, um, perfect track record. So I was a little bit nervous about how I would do. And also it's a quarter system, so basically it's a beginning and an end with no middle. And you screw up for one week and the whole quarter is messed up. So, um, it's like everything has to be well ordered and perfect. I guess another thing that was stressful for me was finals because it was the, um, eleventh week after a ten-week quarter. We had a real short half-week, what's called the reading period, where our teachers aren't supposed to give us any new material. And we just review intensely for the upcoming exams. But it was tough because the finals are cumulative, and, um, you need to be able to incorporate everything you've learned, to, um, solve different problems that they give you on the test.

Interviewer: So how do you deal with that stress when you feel it?

Andrew: Well, one of my friends, before I left, um, told me about a sport called crew, which is basically a four- or eight-man boat. You get in a boat and you row for hours and hours, and so I saw advertisements for the crew team written in chalk on the sidewalk around the campus, so I went to an informational meeting and checked it out. And it seemed pretty good to me, so I joined it. I mean it's really intense physically, but that, um, physical, mental balance . . . it helped me to deal with the stress in a lot of ways.

Henry:

Interviewer: So, Henry, what kinds of things cause you stress, and what do you do about them?

Henry: Um, I think the main things that cause me stress are different kinds of worries, like, um, worries about money, worries about my children, and worries about my work. And I think that the main way that I try to deal with them is by not letting them all collect into a, um, big, impossible, gigantic conglomeration. And instead by trying to take each part, like the money part, and asking . . . um, for example, if I'm having trouble meeting my bills, or I'm having trouble getting enough money together . . . . What are the different things that I can do, and when can I do them to take some action to solve the problem? To keep that separate from worries about my kids and the frantic schedule that I have picking them up and taking them different places and doing things with them and for them and, um, keeping those two things separate from my work schedule and different kinds of, um, aggravations that are happening there. So by taking things separately and looking at things in some kind of order. That seems to be the way that I reduce my worry level, and when I reduce my worry level, I reduce the stress that I feel from those things.

SKILLS INDEX

R = Reading
L = Listening
V = Video

LISTENING & SPEAKING SKILLS

PHOTO CREDITS